DEADLY ART OF SURVIVAL
MAGAZINE DEADLYARTOFSURVIVAL.COM

FOUNDERS

Nathan Ingram, Publisher

Jacob Ingram

Chasity Ingram

STAFF

Editor-in-Chief: Dasun Imanuel

Managing Editor: Glen Beck

Design: Jacob Ingram

Robert Lee Lewis

Blake King

Jacky Fung

Anna Goris

Jennielyn Salmorin

Herman Pride

WRITERS

Robert Shimonski

Diane Wallander

Frank A. Bonanno

Edward "Sunez" Rodriguez

CONTACT US

201-428-0989
551-245-7120
DAS@INGRAMUNIVERSAL.COM
DEADLYARTOFSURVIVAL.COM

TABLE OF CONTENTS

05   **DAOS OPINION**
Be Your Best Self!

07   **KUSHINDA LAMARR THORNTON**
The Godfather of Harlem.

11   **SAMUEL SCOTT**
The Silent Warrior.

17   **TED R. GREEN**
The Mayor of East Orange, NJ.

23   **CEZAR BORKOWSKI**
Canada's Finest.

27   **ERIC JEFFERSON**
Outstanding Martial Artist.

PATREON MEMBERS

1. CHRIS POWELL
2. PAUL CERVIZZI
3. CLARENCE MINNIEFIELD
4. RAN DUM
5. EMMANUEL KIMATHI
6. M TERRY
7. ALDA E ANDUZE
8. HAROLD WHITFIELD
9. MIMI ELLIOTT
10. DAVID JAMES HICKMAN
11. GREG HOLBROOK
12. SHAWN WASHINGTON
13. DARRYL CORDICE
14. KEVIN SMITH
15. CARRIE JOHNSON
16. REYNA ROSS
17. LEROY HINES
18. JETT
19. VALENCIA ROBINSON
20. NAIMAH EL
21. M. LAMB
22. THOMAS LEBRUN
23. NICOLE
24. KEVIN NOTCH
25. JASON VELEZ
26. JONATHAN MEYER
27. BRANDON STAUFT
28. MALIK SHABAZZ
29. FRANCISCO GOMEZ
30. FRANK BONANNO
31. DJ J-RONIN
32. TIMOTHY HOLLYWOOD
33. DAS WARRIOR
34. KENNETH HILL JR
35. KAMU AKIL CHUKWUENEKA
36. SHAKE (THE POET)
37. MARIKA
38. MICHAEL BURNS
39. JAI FARRELL
40. RUFUS PETERSON
41. WAYNE BROWN
42. NIKOLA
43. TONY DIAZ
44. THE MARTIAL MAZE
45. BRIAN J KIESEL
46. OMAR SCHWANZER
47. GARY BORUM
48. GREGORY DUNCAN
49. GREGORY MIDDLETON
50. LOUIS MARKSTROM
51. KAMAL H. MINKAH
52. LOUIS A ECHAVARRIA
53. BRION THORMAN
54. CLAY WORLEY
55. ROBERT SADORA
56. NATHARRIS
57. ROBERTO GARCIA
58. JOSEPH REYES
59. JOHN CUNNINGHAM
60. SALIMAL-RASHID
61. FELIZ R MEJIA III
62. SAMUEL SCOTT
63. JOSEPH RODRIGUEZ ANOO-ELI
64. DWAYNE WINTER
65. GLENN JONES
66. FREDERICK BROOKS
67. WATTS
68. ANTOINE BRAGG
69. SENSEI EMMETT
70. HAISAN KALEAK
71. DEREK MUHAMMAD
72. DANIEL JOSEPHS
73. JAY G.
74. STEPHEN STAFFORD
75. JOHN FITZPATRICK
76. FLORINE THOMPSON
77. PENNY JOHNSON
78. BERNARD USSERY
79. MEKEYTA FREEMAN
80. RICKY HURDLE
81. FRANK POLLARD
82. M. ALEX MEDEL
83. DAVID BLAKE
84. S.H.U.N
85. TERESA TAWWAB

100. LATIFAH MAHDI
101. PHARYLE BODDIE
102. FLORINE THOMPSON
103. VICTOR LASHLEY
104. SWAM ACADEMY OF MARTIAL ARTS
105. C.L.
106. ODETTE RUSSELL
107. TUHON DURAND HOWARD
108. JIHAD BATTLE
109. PRICE GARLAND
110. ED CARRILLO EAGLES MARTIAL ARTS SYSTEM
111. GARY SHARPE
112. HAISAN KALEAK
113. BARAK YALAD
114. CARL MATTHEWS
115. DARRYL STARKS SR
116. DAMIEN WRIGHT
117. LEE SCHWARTZBERG
118. CAMI FERRY
119. NINA

Thank You
to our patreon members for your support!

JOIN OUR PATREON

And invest in what you love!

Register at

Patreon.com/DAOSTV or Deadlyartofsurvival.com

SCAN ME

DAOS REPRESENTATIVES

1. HAISAN KALEAK- NEW YORK
2. RAY RODRIGUEZ - NEW YORK
3. JIM RIVERA- FLORIDA
4. SAMUEL SCOTT- MARYLAND
5. ANTHONY ARANGO-LONG ISLAND
6. JAMES DEBROW-TEXAS
7. DARRYL STARKS SR.- CHICAGO
8. ODETTE RUSSELL-ATLANTA
9. KAMAU AKIL CHUKWUENEKA- KENTUCKY
10. ABDUL SHABAZZ- ATLANTA
11. IVAN MENDEZ-NEW JERSEY
12. NINA BLANCO-PENNSYLVANIA
13. SHI FU GREGG ZILB LONG ISLAND

BUSINESS DIRECTORY
FOR MARTIAL ARTS SCHOOLS & SMALL

NEW YORK- LONG ISLAND

- Frank Bonanno Dai Nan Wan Ryu Ju-Jitsu & Judo 36 Lumur Drive Sayville, New York, 11782 (631) 523-7574 fbonannojr22@gmail.com

FLORIDA

- Coach-John Yarborough Ohana Martial Arts 788 March Street North Fort Myers, FL, 33903 (239) 200-3063

GET YOUR STATE/PLACED HERE

- Get your dojo or small business placed here for thousands to see physically and digitally!

JOIN OUR PATREON

and have your dojo or small business listed in The DAOS Magazine for free!

Register at
Patreon.com/DAOSTV
or
Deadlyartofsurvival.com

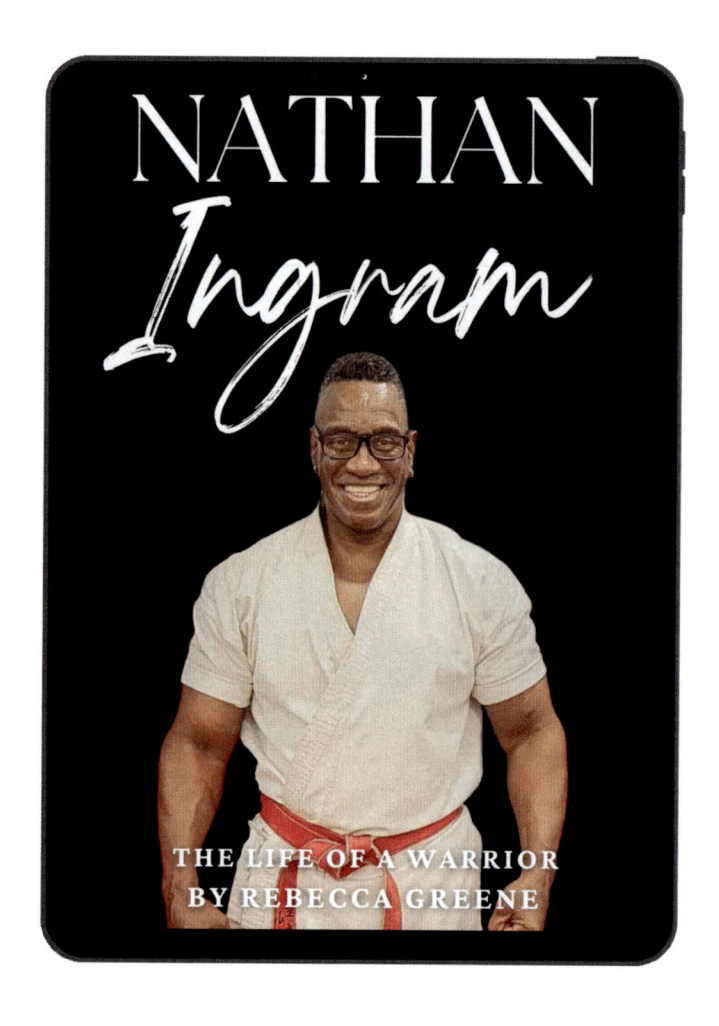

NATHAN Ingram
THE LIFE OF A WARRIOR
BY REBECCA GREENE

available at **amazon**

- Free Online Seminars!
- Earn as an affiliate!
- Free Giveaways!
- Free Ebooks!
- Discounts on magazines!

04 | DEADLYARTOFSURVIVAL.COM

THE DAOS OPINION

BE YOUR BEST SELF

Written by: Shidoshi Nathan Ingram & Shihan Glen Beck

Professionals, amateurs, hobbyists, zealots, fanatics, lunatics, traditionalists, purists, general practitioners, fakers, exaggerators, liars, gymnasts, breakers, fighters, weekend warriors, dancers, rank-seekers, title claimants, award collectors, dojo jumpers, survivalists, and photo takers; these and many more are the makeup of the martial art community.

As well as the seemingly countless categories within our way of life, you will also find many roads and those who walk the thoroughfares within the arts. They're diverse in their mannerisms, beliefs, wants, religions, races, cultures, and even what they offer. Some categories are pleasant and inclusive, while others might be offensive to some. Regardless of their reasons for training, whether good, bad, or even sinister, it's their right to train.

They are all here to stay regardless of which category they might fit into, but only so many will make it to the top of the pyramid. Comparatively and unbelievably, some might 'fake' make it to the pinnacle rank, the difference between the two, however, is obvious to those in the know.

I say this to say that our beloved arts have a wide range of folks within our ranks, and we have to check the boxes that best define who we are, find like-minded practitioners, and avoid the ones who differ from us diametrically of you must. Stop the crap and enjoy the arts as you see fit.

The ideals of honor, discipline, respect, and confidence set long before we were born may have veered off course for some, but it doesn't mean that we have to continue in that fashion. Be the best you can be, and do so knowing that you honor your family lineage.

This is the DAOS OPINION.

Legends

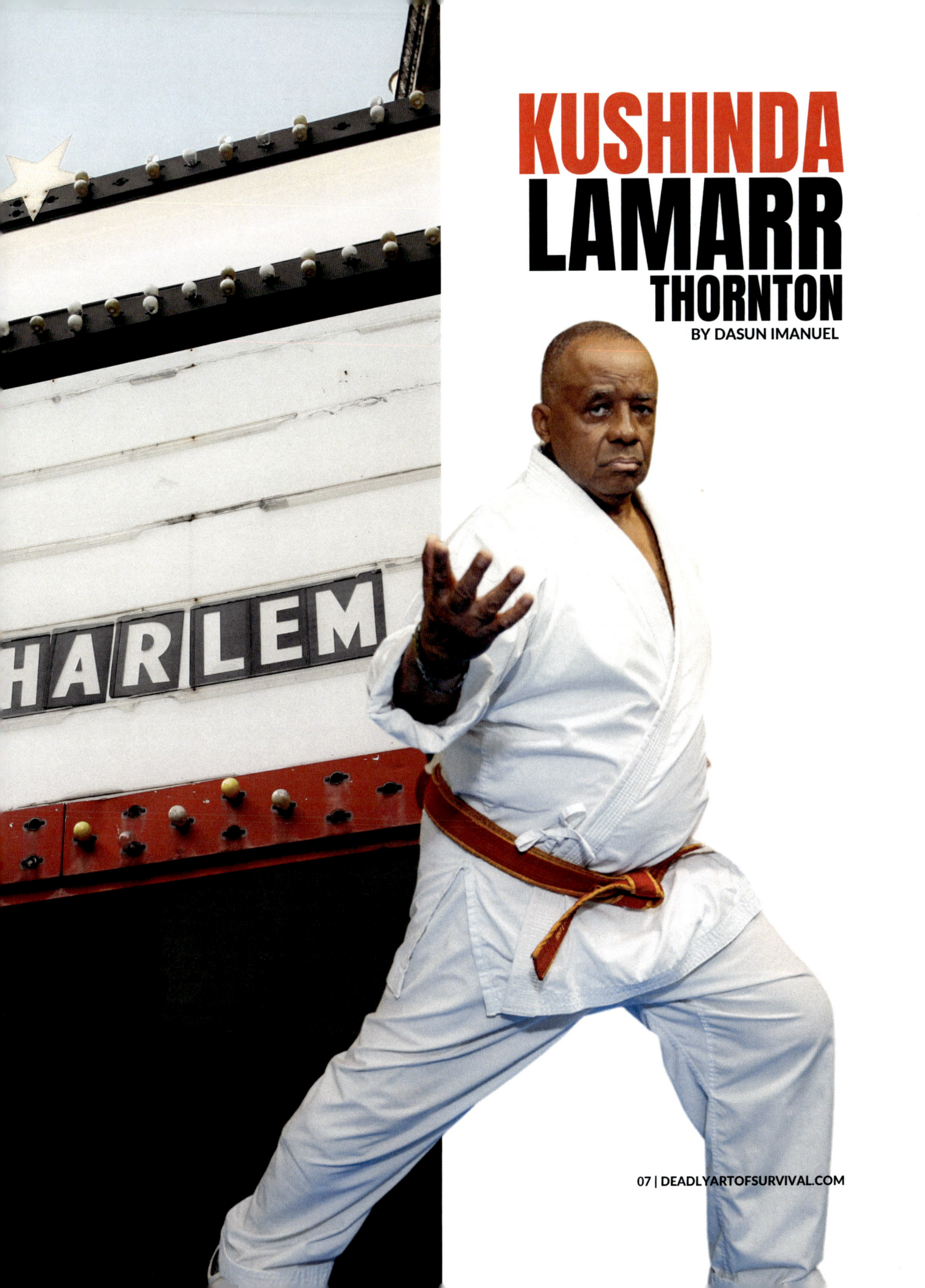

KUSHINDA
LAMARR
THORNTON
BY DASUN IMANUEL

07 | DEADLYARTOFSURVIVAL.COM

Kushinda Lamarr Thornton, known as "The Godfather" of Harlem Martial Arts is a 10th Dan Red Belt and founder of the Kushindaryu Martial Arts System. Thornton has had many accomplishments in his nearly six decades of training. He is a life member of USA Karate and 1992 State Champion of their over 35 division, the New York State Committee Officer of JuJutsu for RSO USA Karate and a prominent promoter of East Coast Martial Arts tournaments in the United States, as well as abroad. He was the Chief Instructor of the NCAA National Youth Sports Program at City College and served 18 years as Tournament Director and Producer for Sports Foundation's Summer Youth Olympics. He has been inducted into countless Halls of Fame including being the recipient of the 1992 All American Karate Hall of Fame Award.

Thornton was instrumental, along with Wesley Snipes' Amen-Ra Films, in producing the Tribute to Martial Arts Masters of the Twentieth Century. His instruction has been influential on notable celebrity martial artists such as Dr. Wesley Snipes and Micheal Jai White. July 19, 2016 was even recognized as "Lamarr Thornton Day" by Charles B. Rangel, retired Dean of The 13th Congressional District of New York. He is the author of Kushindaryu Martial Arts Reverse Knockout Strategy for the Victim and has been responsible for security at annual "Harlem Week" festivities for the past 27 years.

Kushinda Lamarr Thornton was born in May of 1950, in Chattanooga, Tennessee. He came to Harlem in 1958 and remembers it as being a beautiful place. Although there were some bad apples, there were gangs and drugs, that element kept to itself. "The Harlem community during that time was managed by the people in the community," says Thornton. "The person that owned the bakery, Ms. Wilson, the store owners, they kind of controlled the community along with the people that lived in the community." He describes that historic Harlem as being tight-knit and safe due to the relationships between the people and business owners. "I can remember Roy Campanella was a baseball player. I lived right across the street from Roy Campanella's liquor store," says Thornton. "He would stand outside of the store and make sure we stayed in check, and make sure that the kids weren't going crazy. Or if there was a gang fight, everybody in the community, the store owners, they would come out and stop that, they made sure that the gang fights were stopped. Or that there was no confusion going on in the community."

Nevertheless, Thornton faced his challenges. Part of his experience from running the streets at a young age, was being bullied. Thornton found himself frequently fighting in the streets. It was around this time, at the age of nine, that he became acquainted with the martial arts at St. Philip's Church on 134th Street in Harlem. "I was influenced by the director because he used to always see me crying or angry, but I was angry because a lot of times the kids would pick on me, the bullies," says Thornton. "The director, Mr. Edwards, he was very much concerned about most of the kids in the community." Mr. Edwards started a judo program at the church and enrolled young Thornton. The instructor was Grandmaster Chaka Zulu.

"When I first started training with Grandmaster Chaka Zulu, the judo was very hard for me. It wasn't easy, but for some reason or another, I felt like I was safe by doing the training," says Thornton. "Grandmaster Chaka Zulu, he was a very compassionate person; caring. But one thing that they did do that was interesting," says Thornton. "They taught me not to back down through the judo training. They would go out in the streets and get the bad kids, the bullies, and bring them into the class to spar. I remember sparring with one of the baddest kids on the block in judo. He beat me, but I got a little respect because I was able to fight him back."

From there, Thornton moved to The Bronx. His brother's friend Paul Lilly was a student of Grandmaster Thomas Boddie at his Karate Dojo at 163rd Street in Manhattan. Thornton began to train with Lily along with Earl Henderson in Goju Karate. "Those brothers, Earl Henderson and Paul Lilly, we would meet at the schoolyard and play basketball. They invited us to train with them," says Thornton. "They would go to their dojo, train, and then they would come home, come back to the community, and they would train us either in the park or in Earl Henderson's basement. At that time, there were four or five of us that were training. Out of the four of us, I stayed with Paul and Earl, and I started training in Goju."

Eventually, Lilly grew ill and Henderson went into the service. Thornton had no one with whom to study. "I started training out of a book called This is Karate by Masutatsu Oyama; a little small book," says Thornton. "I started training on my own for about two years, maybe three years and then I met Bradford Gonzalez" Thornton was then in the ninth grade and Bradford was a Five Percenter who practiced karate with other Five Percenters. "We would get together in the gym and do techniques on the side. And one day, some kind of way, Bradford found out about Peter Urban," says Thornton. "We went down to Chinatown and walked in and introduced ourselves to Master Peter Urban. He took us right in, sat us down in the office, and we had a long conversation, and he gave us a scholarship. So I trained at Chinatown Dojo on Canal Street, the first dojo." Initially, the scholarship was for the regular class with other youth. "When we got in the class, we were beating the kids up so bad, [Urban] said, 'You guys can't come to my regular class, y'all gotta go to Black Belt.' So he invited us to Black Belt class on Saturday and Sunday. I was with the great masters, the go-to masters of New York." Among the many who were there at the time was Frank Ruiz, Al Gotay, Chris DeBaise, Chaka Zulu, Ulysses Edwards, Rico Guy and Louis Delgado.

In the ensuing years, in addition to Peter Urban and the aforementioned, Thornton was able to train with legendary grandmasters such as Moses Powell and Soke Lil John Davis. "My buddy and I used to compete in the tournaments, whether we made the final or not, we would sit and watch the masters do exhibitions," said Thornton. "And we saw Moses Powell and Lil John Davis bouncing around on the stage. We decided after they did their exhibition to go up and introduce ourselves. Moses Powell, and John Davis said, "Oh, you know, you guys are good. We've been watching you. You can come by the dojo. Make sure you let your instructor know you're going to be coming by the dojo." Though Thornton and his friend lacked finances, when competitions came up, the masters looked out for them constantly. "I've met Aaron Banks, who was one of my other good mentors. We didn't have any money and Aaron and Peter Urban knew," says Thornton. "Mr. Urban would make a phone call to Aaron and tell Aaron, 'look, I got some guys here. They don't have money, but I would like for them to be in a tournament. So during this time, in the 60s, all the way from green belt to about brown belt, I used to go to tournaments. I used to get free scholarships to tournaments from Aaron Banks, Frank Ruiz, Peter Urban and Pete Siringano from Staten Island."

Rigorous is the first word that comes to mind when he thinks of training with Soke Lil John Davis. "John's a very, very kind person when he's off the mat, but when he gets on the mat, it's no joke," says Thornton. "I remember doing 500 jumping jacks before class, 200 or 300 pushups before class. And going through the training and going through the drills, doing the drills over and over again. There's three or four hour classes. Lil John was a super drill instructor." As Thornton speaks on his teachers, it seems that each one contributed different elements that were instrumental in his success.

He describes Grandmaster Moses Powell as a scientist. "He was what you would call a true Grandmaster," says Thornton. "Lil John would warm us up for about an hour and a half and then Grandmaster Moses Powell would come on the mat and then he would train us in the, I don't want to use the word creative techniques, but he would show us how to apply that in JuJutsu," says Thornton. "He would show us, give us the science of JuJutsu." Grandmaster George Cofield was another major influence. "I met Master Cofield through Master Moses Powell because they had a group at one point," says Thronton. "If you were affiliated with Moses Powell's dojo, you were allowed to go train with one of the masters in that particular organization... By that time, I think I was black belt and I had my own dojo at the church. He taught me how to build a dojo, run a dojo, and how to conduct yourself as a teacher and master. He was a serious, tough master, but he [Cofield] was a wizard and a wise man when it came to running a martial arts school."

Another mentor was Grandmaster Thomas LaPuppet. "Sensei LaPuppet taught me how to run tournaments and taught me how to fight. Sensei LePuppet was a gentleman, another extremely professional person," says Thornton. "He was the one that started me out in giving tournaments and he always emphasized diplomacy. He said, 'little brother, you gotta have diplomacy. Don't separate yourself from the people, but you always have to be diplomatic and be kind, respectful of the people if you're going to be a tournament director." Thornton credits Grandmaster Abdul Musawwir, from whom he earned the rank of Master in Yummukwan, as the teacher that taught him the true and right way of doing Shotokan Karate and how to teach martial arts. "Abdul Musawwir was a technician, a master technician. He taught me how to do technique the right way," says Thornton. "It was always very technical in that process. I attribute my teaching skills to him. He taught me how to teach. Abdul Musawwir was my teaching instructor."

After teaching with the Police Athletic League (PAL) and in churches, Thornton opened up his first dojo, New Breed Dynamic Youth Association, in 1974 on 183rd Street in The Bronx. Since then, the name has gone through many changes and is currently known as New Breed Life Arts and Educational Association and located at 233 West 135th Street in Harlem. "I had support from the PAL. They gave me free reign to do whatever I wanted to do and do whatever I needed to do," says Thornton. He savors that early experience of having the freedom to set standards and develop the way he was going to teach and present his program.

He recalls his days of organizing tournaments with a reserved fondness. "I've always liked to see people come together and have an experience of sharing and carrying on information or being in competition. That was what I really enjoyed about tournaments," says Thornton. "Martial arts tournaments are not easy to put together. It's a lot, a lot of work and you have to really have a lot of patience, because you're dealing with all different kinds of personalities. But the beautiful thing about doing martial arts tournaments, you can get a chance to see all the different styles and skills. When you give a good tournament, a big tournament, and you get all these different styles and skills, you see all these different techniques. It's unbelievable to see people move the way they move. And when I was coming up, the fighting was like, it's like going to the movies and seeing a Kung Fu movie."

That same fondness is reflected in his recollections of his competitive days. "New York was the Mecca of martial arts globally," says Thornton "You would look up at Madison Square Garden in the tournament during the time when [Shidoshi Nathan Ingram] and I were coming up in the sixties and early seventies, and you would meet someone or you would face off with someone from Bulgaria or from Japan or from China." He says he was honored to have fought some of the great masters of his time. He had many wins, but also suffered some losses. "Most of the time when I didn't make the finals or lost the championship, is because I didn't do the proper training," says Thornton. "The key is training, proper diet and you got to be in good shape."

The culmination of his studies in martial arts and related sciences was the development of his own style, Kushindaryu, which means "strategic method." It is based on the spiritual foundation of high consciousness and is a combination of Tai Chi Yoga, Shotokan Karate, Goju Karate and JuJutsu, along with karate boxing, and strategic fighting tactics. The system incorporates yoga as well as special breathing and mental conditioning exercises. When formulating the style, Thornton was familiar with the Japanese terminology, but he wanted his training to relate to his own ancestors. He picked up a book on Kiswahili and researched the language of strategy and came up with the term, "Kushinda," which means chief strategist and added the Japanese word, "Ryu," for way, school or style. The art of Kushindaryu is the way of the chief strategist. "The styles under the art," says Thornton, "are the styles that I study. Shotokan, Goju, JuJutsu, Tai Chi, Yummukwan, Korean Karate, under Abdul Musawwir Munroe. Those are the styles, and I made black belt in Judo, and of course I practice meditation and breathing. You have to master meditation and breathing."

He views the spiritual and psychological aspects of martial arts as very important, but often confused. "Sometimes a lot of us, a lot of us master's too, misunderstand martial arts as being a religion. It's not a religion. It's a way of life. The styles make the way of life," says Thornton. "The spiritual, the mental and the physical, one cannot dowithout the other. You can't say that you're a spiritual martial artist without dealing with programs literally and physically. This is a holistic issue. It's a holistic program, not from a spooky perspective, not from a religious perspective, but from a natural, life skills perspective." Thornton's New Breed Life Arts and Educational Association emphasizes building character, discipline and non-violence. "Non-violence doesn't necessarily mean you walk around and let people beat the hell out of you," says Thornton. "Non-violence means that you're not, in our philosophy, the aggressor or you're not the instigator." But if someone touches you, Thornton's training definitively teaches one how to defend and evade.

After 58 years, Kushinda Lamarr Thornton is showing no signs of slowing down. He continues to be a force in the Harlem community committed to education through martial arts and promoting non-violence and discipline. It is a mission of "saving lives and changing lives, one child at a time, one family at a time, and then, bringing all families together." It is his lifelong mission and a legacy that will live on long after he is gone.

GM
SAMUEL SCOTT

BY DASUN IMANUEL

11 | DEADLYARTOFSURVIVAL.COM

Grandmaster Samuel Scott describes January 29, 2022, as the day his life turned upside down. GM Scott, a 9th-degree Black Belt and practitioner of the arts since 1975, had spent 29 years teaching at his 8,000 sq ft facility in the Prince George's County area of Maryland. Then, a phone call came in the middle of the night.

It was around 1:20 am on the morning of the 30th, and his sister-in-law, Guro Johanna Williams, was telling him the school was on fire and urging him to get there. Scott minimized the situation in his mind. "Because it was a brick building," says Scott, "I was getting the impression that she was just talking about maybe somebody might have thrown something through the window, and the front area was on fire." But the closer he got to the facility, the more black smoke he saw filling the air. When he arrived on the scene, he says it looked like The Towering Inferno. The school was totally engulfed in flames and two fire companies were there fighting the blaze. "They had those cranes," says Scott. "One was in the front, one was in the back, and they were shooting water down into my school. The entire roof collapsed. You might say the place burned to the ground."

Scott lost everything. He had special achievement awards from Grandmasters whom he held in high regard, irreplaceable as they are all deceased. Special gifts from China, Abu Dhabi, and Panama, where he has trained special forces and law enforcement, are now incinerated. Scott had over 300 fights on the national circuit and kept some of his favorite trophies to remind him of his notable wins and losses, all destroyed. "I had masters who made suits for me, uniforms for me. I had weapons that were given to me as gifts. All of that was burned to the ground. All my certificates, my life skill coaching certificates, everything." He says no one knows how deeply hurt he felt that day. After speaking with the fire inspector, he went home and stared into space for hours before he finally fell asleep...

An avalanche of accolades and accomplishments accompany the ascension of Grandmaster Samuel Scott upon the mountain of martial arts mastery. He has studied the styles of Tien Shen Pai Kung Fu, Filipino martial arts, Tai Chi/Chi Kung, Chin Na, Kyusho Jitsu, and Gracie Ground Tactics, among other disciplines. He is the founder of Combat Kuntao International, the Full Circle Martial Arts Academy, Elite Training Group, Warriors Against Trafficking, the 10X Martial Arts Business Group, co-founder of The Women's Personal Safety Network, and the author of eight books. He is a member of NAPMA, the National Association of Professional Martial Artists, and the World Head Sokeship Council, and he was inducted into their Hall of Fame in 1995 as "Instructor of the Year" and with a Founders Award in 2005. Scott is the recipient of the "Living Legend Award" from the late Grandmaster Robert Everhart in Nippon Kenpo Karate and the "Pioneer Award" from the late Grandmaster Reggie Jackson. He received his "Master" credentials from the late Nganga Tolo Na in 1997 and received the title of Grandmaster from Ama Guro Raffy Pambuan in 2017. One of his most cherished, however, is the "Living Legend" award he recieved from *Deadly Art of Survival*, the first award he acquired after the destruction of his dojo.

Scott has taught thousands of students, has promoted 165 Black Belts, and produced four masters. He trained the Special Force and Diplomat Escort Teams of the Panama Police and provided edged-weapon training to the US Air Force Special Tactics Squadron. It's always a defining moment when teaching super soldiers. An instructor must earn their respect. "I was the last trainer to come in to teach them edged weapons," says Scott. He had showed up early to get a feel for the atmosphere and overheard the soldiers talking, anticipating the training. "I like to be invisible in their presence, just to kind of hear the unheard," says Scott. The colonel, who usually slips in and out, stayed for most of the presentation. After teaching them the fundamentals, Scott went into his bag for felt-edged "virtual blades," which leave a chalk mark where strikes are applied.

"I started showing them how to defend against an edge weapon, and then they had to do a live scenario where they would actually be attacked by the guys with these chalk blades," says Scott. "They were getting cut up all on the vital areas of their bodies. But by the time we finished the training, many of them went through and didn't get hit in the vital area because of the defense I was teaching them, and you can kind of see the kid come out of them. Getting really excited and inspired by it." The colonel was so impressed that he wanted to renew the training, specifically with GM Scott at the helm. "My focus has always been on reality; it's all I know, " says Scott. "I gear my training towards 'what-if' scenarios. When you talk about niche, that's where I feel my niche is because I'm always finding and refining the what-if factor."

Since 2014, with his Elite Training Group, Scott was able to secure a multi-year contract with several agencies of the United Arab Emirates (UAE). Dubai is the central hub, but the training took place in Abu Dhabi. "The training was interesting because we had to teach them the use of force. So it was a week of classroom, which is soft skills, and then a week of hard skills, which was hand-to-hand compliance and control tactics, as well as firearms," says Scott. "They don't really have crime in their area, so they weren't really up to speed on any of the training; even their fitness level wasn't as good. We were pressed by the admin command staff to get them in some type of physical shape. All in all, it was good, though. We were the only African-American training group there in the UAE. There's about 200 training groups there, from what I understand, and they evaluated each training group every cycle. And we were the number one training group consistently."

Because of their performance, Elite Training Group received a renewal every time a new contract arose. But even more than that, Scott and his team's training inspired a legacy. "We taught the investigator's team there. We taught the traffic police and homicide detectives. And then we went there and taught the special task teams who are responsible for special events. And we taught the dignitary escort, which is like the secret service of the U.S.," says Scott. "The gentleman who's in charge of the special task team is now in charge of the martial arts program there. He calls himself my student. I accept him as my student, actually, but we were very good friends."

A couple of months ago, the gentleman invited him down and brought him to a facility. "I had no idea where we were going... He brought me to this building. When we opened the door up, it was about a hundred officers in there training martial arts," says Scott. "He said, 'This is what you all inspired.' He said, 'The government now has an official martial arts training program, and this building is designed strictly for the martial arts training program.' And so I'm kind of looking, and I was humbled by it because I really had no idea that the training we did actually encouraged them to start a martial arts program." The gentleman also proposed that Scott oversee the martial arts training in Abu Dhabi.

14 | DEADLYARTOFSURVIVAL.COM

The man who became Grandmaster Samuel Scott was born in 1961 in Hempstead, NY, and grew up in Gordon Heights. "Typical tough neighborhood," says Scott. "One of the reasons why I started martial arts was just to be able to defend myself against the bullies and the other folks in the neighborhood in school. We didn't have much to do. It was like we had a little park that everybody went to." Scott describes the stereotypical urban playground set-up replete with the requisite basketball hoop with no net. "You just went there, and you just played basketball. You fight. You play basketball. You fight," says Scott. He began his self-described enlightening and fulfilling journey in martial arts 49 years ago as of this writing.

"I've always been fascinated with martial arts since I was six, seven years old. My parents couldn't really afford to put me in class. But I'd always go look at those old school movies, *Five Fingers of Death* and all those different movies," says Scott. "So I would go down and pay 25 cents, sit in the theater all day long, and watch. Then Bruce Lee came along, and that was the game changer for me. And so I said, 'I got to seek out an instructor.'" Scott linked up with a gentleman in the neighborhood who taught Taekwondo and began his study. As he matured, he set out to go to trade school in Texas. It was there that he began studying Kung Fu under Shifu Tee Gums. "He was from Jamaica. Phenomenal, phenomenal martial artist. I was 16 at the time," says Scott. "It just never stopped after that just always; wherever I went, I always sought out a school to train in the arts. I'm a fanatic."

He recalls his early training as being unlike anything that is commonplace today. It was rigid and straight, no-nonsense. "There wasn't a lot of talking in class. You worked the same technique until you almost passed out. And I think it gave me a solid foundation in training. All those reps let me know how valuable the basics were. Because as a kid, you don't want no basics. You want to learn how to fly and all that kind of stuff," says Scott. "So, all those reps conditioned me subconsciously to focus on the one technique or two techniques and rep them things out to second nature."

From Texas, Scott moved to the greater Washington, DC area, known as DMV for DC, Maryland, and Virginia. It was there that he received his first exposure to training in Wing Chun with Shifu Charles Martin. Scott describes Martin's approach as non-traditional and that he taught Scott how to use the art from a reality-based, self-defense perspective. He continued training with Martin for a few years, and then Martin left the area. "I didn't want to do anything but Wing Chun. I was hooked!" says Scott. "But there wasn't a Wing Chun instructor in the area. So after about a year or two, I had to go find something." It was around 1985 when he went to the school of Grandmaster Dennis Brown. "I planted there," says Scott. "I got my black under him." He called Lao Shi Dennis Brown's school "home," and there he learned "the graceful art of Kung Fu" and became a top competitor on the tournament circuit in sparring under the tutelage of Grandmaster Ervin Gephart.

After this, Scott ventured into the Filipino arts. By then, he worked as a corrections officer in the DMV area prison system. "My focus has always been combative arts," says Scott. "Traditional arts was fine. Kung fu was fine, and I was doing it during my competition days. But for me, it's always been combative arts, something that I could use in a real-life situation." For Scott, Filipino arts definitely fell into that category. He started being taught privately by Ama Guro Billy Bryant in the deadly art of Kuntaw. Although he did the traditional stick work, his focus was on the empty hand, wresting and grappling, rope art, as flexible weapons are useful in the street, and edged weapons. Scott credits Bryant for giving him a solid foundation in the principles and concepts of art. He trained privately under Bryant for a number of years. Afterward, he trained with Ama Guro Raffy Pambuan, who expanded his knowledge of Filipino martial arts.

Scott says Pambuan's ability to break down the key components of the different arts sped up his learning curve, and Scott's own top instructors and students also had the opportunity to study with Pambuan.

In the mid-90s, it was Pambuan who inspired Scott to create his own style of martial arts. "He came to me one day and said, 'You know you need to start your own Filipino martial arts, right? And I was humbled by that," says Scott. But it was something I would never do, of course. I'm not Filipino, for one. Although I give him credit for that, for the foundation of the art, I think my creativity or my expression of the art didn't originate in the Filipino art. And so he named my art Talahib Kuntao and made it an official thing. He's a fifth-generation head of his family system." Scott took that and named it Combat Kuntao, combat fist way. Among the many other masters that have had an impact on his life are Mufundshi Bakari Alexander. Scott says that everything he knows about the internal arts systems stems from the solid foundation that Mufundshi Bakari gave him. Scott says that although Alexander's physical skills were impeccable, it was his knowledge and wisdom of the arts and life in general that inspired him the most. Scott's commitment to the internal arts manifested in his "Breathing For Life" programs that focused on reducing stress and increasing health. He credits GM Evan Pantazi with providing a framework for his practice of Kyusho Jitsu and GM Bobby Taboada, with whom he and his top instructors had the honor and privilege to train with privately in Balintawak, for influencing his understanding and philosophy of reality fighting. He says that one sit-down conversation with Taboada is worth a year of physical training with some others. He was also able to train in Silat with Dan Inosanto. "There were no schools back then," says Scott. "Silat was new and he was bringing that to the U.S. and so the only way you could learn it was through him at the seminars."

In 1992, Scott was among the top 10 nationals in Atlantic City, along with GM Jerry Fontanez. Scott had won his division, and Fontanez won his. Scott had observed that martial arts schools in his area were tournament-driven, and the champions were the ones that had the school. "I felt like in order for me to open the school up, I had to be a champion. I had to be one of the top three, top five heavyweights. And so I just kept competing, kept winning, competing, kept winning," says Scott. "So we're out having lunch. My wife was with me and a couple of students, and Jerry had about five or six of his students, and they all had their own schools," says Scott. "And so we were talking, and Jerry was talking about schools and strategies and things like that. He turned to me and said, 'How many schools do you have? And I said, 'No, I got to put some more work in.' He said, 'Put some more work in? He said, 'you're winning everything out here. He said, 'You got to!'" Scott recalls his wife rolling her eyes at him as an "I told you so" gesture.

After they parted ways, Scott set his sights on opening up a school. His idea was to enter the International Police Olympics where fighters came from all around the whole wide world of law enforcement, win the gold medal, do a press release and use the notoriety to launch the school. "I went there the day before when they were doing the parades to scope out the competition, and it was a lot. The next day, the line looked like a cheese line in the division," says Scott. "Long story short, went through each match, fought everybody, won each division, won the gold medal, came back and said, 'I'm going to do an article now called "Fighting for the Kids."'" He thought the positive story of his life in the arts and law enforcement would be encouraging to the youth of the community, but there were no takers in the media.

16 | DEADLYARTOFSURVIVAL.COM

"I started calling the news station. I had zero knowledge about how they interact with news media and all. I just got on the phone and shared my story," says Scott. "They didn't want to hear that, man. That's when I learned that the media was all about negative news." A friend of his managed to get Scott's story published in *The Journal of Maryland*, where his friend's mother worked. On February 23rd of 1993, Scott launched his school in his basement with his then business partner GM Wallace Powell and their sons. After six years, he retired from his 15-year-career in corrections without notice, a move that would forfeit $15,000 in benefits. But Scott was determined and his director was so impressed that he allowed him to keep the pay despite the lack of notice. From the basement, Scott's Full Circle Martial Arts Academy flourished at the location that would be its home for the 29 years. And then tragedy struck. After the fire Scott remembers strangers from the community stopping in the parking lot and crying. "I've never experienced that before. Students, yes. Parents, yes. Former parents, yes.

But strangers were pulling over and coming to the parking lot and crying," says Scott. "You don't even know the impact you have in your community until something like that happens." Scott was able to salvage one thing close to his heart, the Blackbelt Wall of Fame plaque which had the names of every blackbelt the school had produced. He pulled it off the wall, wiped it down, and put it in his vehicle. Within 48 hours, he had a temporary location. When Scott arrived at the temporary office space, he recalls every Blackbelt was standing in line like warriors waiting for the order. It was a gust of wind under his wings. Within five days he had a new location two minutes away from the one that burned down. Thus began the process he called, "Building Back Better." Now two years at his new location, Scott continues to focus on the youth and the community that showed him how much of an impact he really had when he went through his fire ordeal. But no matter what, he remains grounded. "At the end of the day, after 49 years, it doesn't matter what title I carry. I appreciate all of them," says Scott. "But at the end of the day, I'm just a student of the arts."

SHIHAN TED R. GREEN

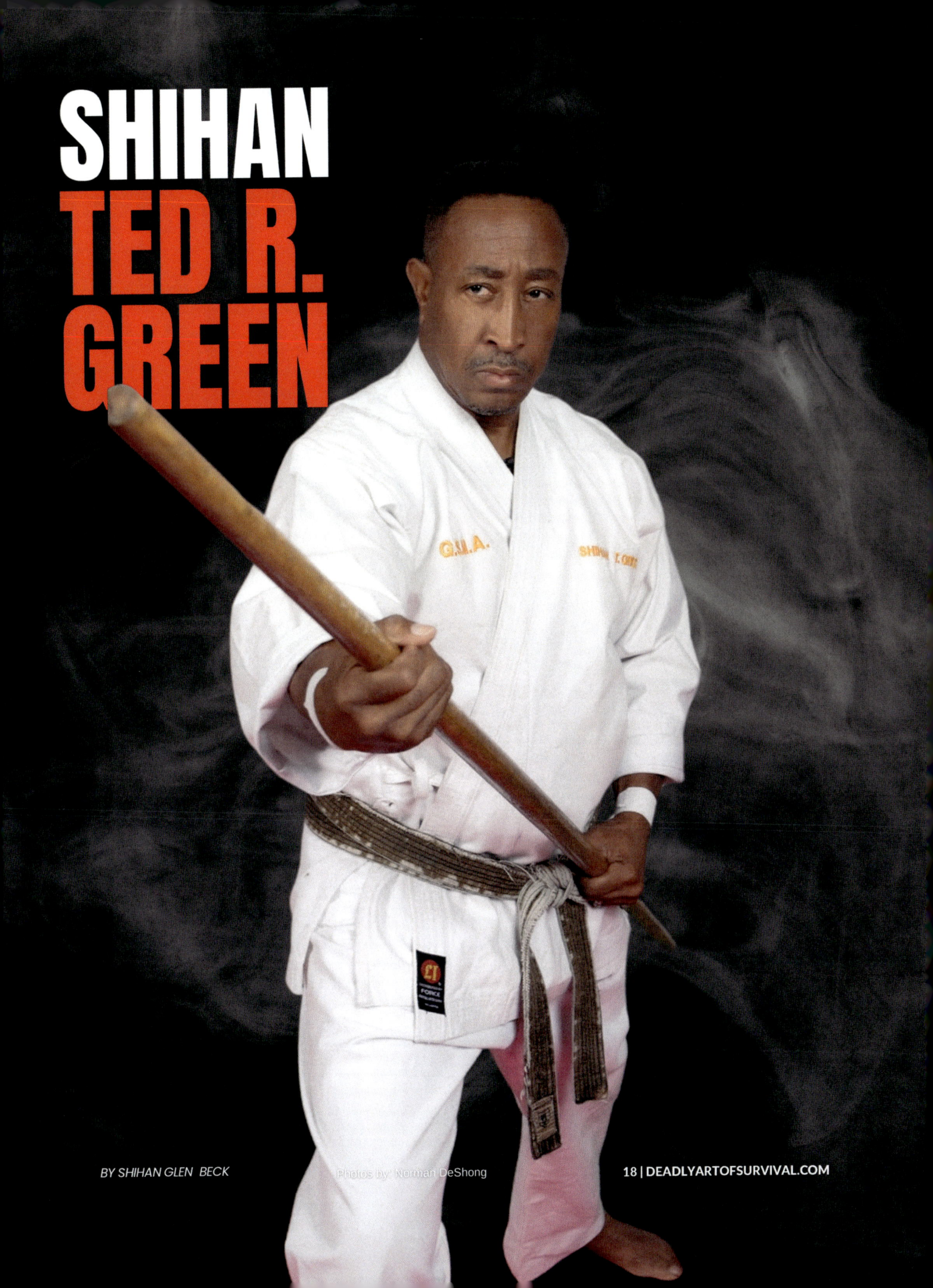

BY SHIHAN GLEN BECK

Photos by: Norman DeShong

18 | DEADLYARTOFSURVIVAL.COM

In every neighborhood, there will always be that special someone who everyone knows. These people can walk or show up anywhere without an invitation and just be accepted. Generally, these notable and easily recognized folks are known as "The Mayor."

There's a man I've been chatting with, and by wild chance, he's known by everyone in the entire city. Obviously, they call him Mr. Mayor. However, unlike most established figures in the neighborhood, this guy was actually voted in by the people to run their city. Please allow me to introduce the Mayor of East Orange, New Jersey, Ted R. Green III.

He was born in 1963 in Newark, New Jersey, and raised in East Orange. When speaking about East Orange, he said, "It was a great experience, neighborhood, and family-oriented. It's the type of place where friends became family; we'd just walk into someone's house without knocking. If it was lunch or dinner time, you were fed. It was a neighborhood, not a hood."

As mayor, with both hands, he holds onto and shares his own childhood memories and experiences while using them as the building blocks of his continued vision of a better life for all. The community life and activities he was exposed to while growing up were filled with adult men who embraced the area youngsters and taught them about life. While no place is perfect, he admits that some committed light robberies or crimes, yet it was still the type of community that most dream about. It was a place where the corner stores knew Mom by name, and parents would pay the bill at the end of the week.

Ted's martial arts career started early, and he's spent a lifetime perfecting it. Beginning with judo at five years old, his first sensei was Dad, Ted R. Green II, who learned from Grandad, a decorated World War II combat veteran.

At first, Dad's dojo was the garage, the backyard, or the park. Each day, they trained wherever it worked best. He had them warming up, stretching, kicking, doing throws, and taking falls in the grass. Eventually, Dad opened the Green School of Martial Arts, a dojo to call their own. All of his students were local kids from the neighborhood who studied the Kuji Kari system, which was a combination of judo, kung fu, and, eventually, Shotokan.

Sensei was old school and definitely the type of man that young Ted could look up to, not just because he was his father. Dad didn't smoke, drink, or do drugs; he was also the living embodiment of an educator. Specifically, he was an elementary school science and special education teacher, one who was loved by all.

Training in the arts was a way of life for Ted and the lessons he learned helped strengthen his inner drive to do his best in all things. Taking a page from Dad's playbook, he enrolled in Cheyney State University, located in Pennsylvania, where he studied and received a degree in business administration. Much later in life, in 2014, he returned to college and ended with a degree in sociology from Lincoln University. The educational ladders that he climbed, along with the experiences he was afforded during those years, helped to form him into the leader he's become today, as well as his life's trajectory in politics coupled with a sincere and innate want to help people.

In 1986, he began taking the steps to give him the additional exposure he would need to lead East Orange successfully.

His first job in government was Housing and Policy Planning and Development, where he redeveloped existing and otherwise run-down homes and community areas.

By '91, Mayor Cordell Cooper offered him a job as the compliance officer for the city of East Orange. Ted Green was gaining a solid understanding of the inner workings of all municipal management programs that he would need to run an American city successfully. Every new job was a step up, including becoming a councilman for 12 years, three times between 2005 and 2017.

While this story is about the life and times of Ted R. Green- the mayor, it's also about the man who would become Grandmaster Green. Looking back, in 1991, at 28 years old, Dad promoted him to 1st-degree black belt, the first of many to come.

As the years move on and maturity sets in, we take on the responsibilities of many things: work, marriage, family, children, and those who are warriors- martial arts. Although the arts are important, oftentimes, these extracurriculars come last on the list of 'wants versus needs' and quickly slow down in the mirror of life's self-growth. It's not something that everyone can continue to keep in their lives, but Ted wasn't everyone. He added as much to his plate as possible and kept his eye on more than one prize. Being a dad, martial artist, good citizen, leader, and mayor was prewritten at the top of the accomplishments printed indelibly in his memoir long before he began to pen the work of his life.

Ted had many people pulling for him to become the successful man he is today. Some he knew, and those whom Ted only knew of who inadvertently gave him the parameters of greatness to follow. Respectfully, reverently, he said the names of Muhammed Ali, calling him "bold, daring and poetic," W. E. B. Du Bois, Marcus Garvey, Martin Luther King, and dear friend Ron Salahuddin- a former Newark Deputy Mayor and master of the Bando martial arts system who pushed him headlong into politics. Over time in the arts, he proved himself to be worthy of many achievements, eventually being promoted by Dad to 6th-degree; by Grandmaster Richard "Rick the Brick" Mayers, he received a 6th-Dan in ninjutsu, and in Sanuces Ryu Jiujitsu, he was promoted to black belt by Professor Ernest Miles. Master Green was a fighter for the people by the people on the stage of politics, and on the mat, he once won the PKA middleweight championship.

Dad didn't like politics but loved, respected, and appreciated the man his son turned out to be, the people's champion. In this, he knew his son had chosen the right profession, one he would excel at doing because of his altruism.

On January 1, 2018, he was sworn in as the 14th Mayor of the City of East Orange after winning an overwhelming 96.6% of the vote. In his second term, he went unopposed due to his overwhelming victory the first time. June 2025, the opportunity to become mayor is up for grabs once again; however, as of now, no challengers have raised their hands and filed to enter the fray. It looks like he'll soon be sworn in as mayor for a third term. I even posed the question, "Governor Green?" He quickly replied, "God willing."

When he first took office, there were some 1000 plus vacant homes in the city of East Orange, which, due to his governing and policies, is now down to approximately 125. Four years back, he created a successful first-time home buyer's program to assist citizens in attaining their American dream by working with the banks. These and many of his other policies came to fruition by being in the streets, going block to block, knocking on doors, and socializing with his constituents while personally asking what they think the city needs. He makes it his business to be visible and reachable, even in the schools extending his hand to the next generation of leaders and voters. These interactions have helped to dub him "The People's Mayor.

He said of the legacy that he hopes to leave for all to see, "It would never have been possible without the family unit that gave me the parameters to live within. The faith in God from my mother and grandmother, who prayed for me daily, who taught me that spirituality feeds the soul of a man, righteousness from my father and grandfather- to be honorable, self-reliant, and to serve my fellow man as if he were my own blood, and the community that raised me which taught me about the 'village' and how the phrase 'Each one, teach one,' is how we grow," says Green. The life lessons he's acquired are the ingredients to an ever-growing system of his existence and help to sharpen his gaze upon the never-ending goals of helping him to advance his family community. You see, he views his constituents and their children as his extended family- and they are about 80,000 in number.

Mayor Ted R. Green has been happily married to First Lady June Green for 29 years. He's the proud father of Eric Lamar (40) and Salahuddin (39), both of whom trained in the arts and are brown belts and black belts, respectively. To this day, he spends his precious time split between his immediate family, governing, and teaching the arts at his dojo, the Green School of Martial Arts. Every Tuesday and Thursday evening, he loves instructing and seeing his young students become respectful adults. Two of his longtime students are on his personal protection detail, and he says, "I know I'm safe when they are around." He even knows how to separate his life: inside the dojo, he's "Shihan," outside of it, he's "Mr. Mayor"; other times, he's "Bee I," a term of endearment given by his four grandchildren. What it derives from no one knows, but it's an honorific that he proudly and lovingly embraces.

GM FRANK BONANNO

JUDO & JU-JUTSU CLASSES

GET IN TOUCH
+631-523-7574

JOIN OUR MARTIAL ARTS CLASSES NEAR BY YOUR LOCATION NOW!

SATURDAY 2 PM - 4 PM
36 LUMUR DRIVE
SAYVILLE NY 11782

JOIN NOW!

21 | DEADLYARTOFSURVIVAL.COM

HAYASHI
CEZAR BORKOWSKI

BY SENSEI ROBERT SHIMONSKI

In a world full of martial artists, few stand out with a lifetime of achievements quite like Hanshi Cezar Borkowski. When asked about Karate, Cezar will tell you, "Karate is who I am. I will die with my Gi on." To understand the depth of knowledge contained within this man and why he relentlessly pursues his passion for martial arts, the first step is to start at the beginning where Cezar first learned about Karate.

Born in 1956 communist Warsaw Poland, Cezar and his family would move to Toronto Canada when he was 10 in December of 1966. The youngest of three older brothers, his upbringing was an early primer in grit and perseverance. "I was kind of self-raised. My mother worked two jobs and my father moved to Canada when I was 5, so between my brothers and I, we had to be self-reliant." This self-reliance would prove to be the foundation on top of which Cezar grew an empire.

Once the family arrived in Toronto, there were some adjustments to be made a new way of life and it was at this time that an unfocused Borkowski, walking the streets looking for something to do, would pass by the front window of a local YMCA offering Karate classes. Immediately intrigued by what he saw taking place inside the local Y's walls, Cezar made an immediate inquiry within. Borkowski was offered a free membership as a benefit to new immigrants in the area and got to take the introductory Karate program. Not realizing it at the time, this one step would ultimately put him on a course on which he would spend a lifetime. Cezar immediately got to work learning Karate. From 1966 until 1971, he continued his training at the local Y. As an immigrant who spoke little to no English, he knew that he needed to get involved in the community and do something of use and this seemed like a great fit. It was, in fact, exactly what he needed to keep him busy and focused.

The class was led by a young woman named Sensei Judy. Judy can be attributed as Borkowski's first official instructor where he learned the basics of self-defense and a series of kata grounded in Wado-ryu. Although his tenure with Judy was short lived, as she soon left the Y, it was at this point that he worked briefly with David Usher learning Chito-ryu. During this time, David would connect Borkowski to Sensei Monty Guest who was a head instructor at master Tsurouka's north branch and at Kai Shin Karate. This is where Borkowski took root and really started to develop his Karate. These humble beginnings would prove to develop Borkowski's fundamental Karate skills into much more than he could imagine.

The foundation already laid; Borkowski really started to develop his advanced skills under Tsurouka Masami. Tsurouka, sometimes referred to as the "Father of Canadian Karate," became a role model and inspiration in Cezar's teenage years all the way through adulthood. In 2014, Tsurouka sensei awarded Borkowski his 9th Hanshi certificate before passing away shortly after. However, there is a lot that would take place between those years. Once he began training under Tsurouka and as the years passed, the drive and ambition to learn more about the martial arts began to grow exponentially. This paved the way towards Cezar not only learning under dozens of other martial arts legends, but also creating one of the most successful schools in Canada today.

While continuing to study at Tsurouka's hombu dojo (head dojo) in Toronto, Borkowski embarked on travels throughout the world to learn more about Karate. Driven by excellence, he would find himself starting his own system and open his first dojo in 1972. Borkowski established his dojo "Northern Karate" and system "Northern Karate System (NKS)" which since started in the 70's has evolved into 15 full time schools in Ontario with over 11,000 students enrolled and learning NKS both in Canada and abroad. "I wanted to bring Karate to the community and to the world. From being an immigrant with very little, my goal was to bring Karate to those and inspire them as it helped inspire and shape me as a youth." Borkowski's NKS offers not only a thorough curriculum of traditional Okinawan Karate and Kobudo, but also heavily modernized grappling arts, boxing, and Silat.

23 | DEADLYARTOFSURVIVAL.COM

Borkowski also focused heavily on both philosophy and understanding the psychology of Karate and its evolution throughout the years. "When developing NKS, there needed to be a focus on differentiating between traditional, sport and social Karate," says Borkowski. He ensures that those who want to learn traditional Okinawan Karate are able to do so. However, those looking more to focus on competition and competing in sport Karate tournaments are provided that path to follow. "For those who are young and want to test themselves, sport Karate is perfect for them," says Borkowski. The theory behind this is, as they grow and want to learn more traditional Karate, then they can do that and this provides a lifelong path for them, but also evolves as they do. "Traditional Karate focused work is great for anyone and everyone,' says Borkowski. "'For example, a 60-year-old can start Karate as a white belt and learn movement, mobility, stay fit and develop their strength while learning a new art."

Then there is the social aspect of Karate. This is where those who are looking for a group, team or outlet can come and join Karate and have and set goals, build with their community, and give back through charity as examples. "At NKS, we are focused on ensuring that we are already involved with charity and giving back to the community. As an example, we worked with a local school in the past where we provided Karate classes to students at a low cost, but in the end took all proceeds that we collected and gave it back to the school in order to provide the students and the school help in areas where they needed it. We have also worked with food banks, raising money for cancer awareness and other notable charities to help develop social Karate."

While Borkowski worked to build NKS, he never stopped learning as a student. Throughout the 80's and up until today, he has traveled the world learning more about the arts. This served the purposes of not only developing himself as a martial artist, but also to help to continue to grow NKS into what it is today. "NKS's evolving curriculum reflects my own continuing martial arts journey, and while on the surface it might appear to be a departure from Okinawan martial traditions, it's my opinion that it also mirrors the path that masters like Miyagi, Kyan and Motobu would follow if they were alive today." Through those travels, Borkowski found how to build on what he had learned but also find a great balance on what works and what does not. When you think about how many influential instructors, masters and leaders in martial arts he has worked with, it truly is mind blowing to say the least.

As Borkowski continued his journey through the years, by the mid-1980's, he was busy building NKS, learning other styles to help augment his knowledge and traveling aboard in order to do so. It was during this time that he made his first trip to Okinawa, to visit 'the Birthplace of Karate-do'. Other trips included, but are not limited to, mainland Japan, China, India, Thailand, Cambodia, Vietnam, Malaysia, Indonesia and Singapore. When asked, he proudly tells the story that "for nearly a quarter of a century, I have been fortunate to train with and develop strong ties with Matayoshi Shinpo, Akamine Eisuke, Hokama Tetsuhiro, Nagamine Soshin, Nagamine Takayoshi, Nakazato Jyoen, Higa Seikichi, Kinjo Masakazu, Kishaba Chogi, Miyazato Eiko, Gakiya Yoshiaki, Nakamoto Masahiro, Tomimoto Yuko, Nakasone Kenzo, and the Shacho of Shureido, as well as cordial relationships with others, like Sakumoto-sensei and the Shinjo brothers." From these teachings he has been able to not only develop himself, but also pass on these lessons to others he has taught.

Borkowski was also a member, and later Canadian Director, for IMAF/Kokusai Budoin of Japan, and trained with masters like Sato sensei, Kanazawa sensei, Yamaguchi sensei, and Kai sensei. "Although Kai Kuniyuki sensei, a Goju-ryu 8th dan, actually encouraged me to travel to Okinawa, my first trip to Asia led me to my wife, Marion," says Borkowski. While following his martial arts journey, he was also incredibly blessed to find his Wife Marion Manzo, a former national champion and 9th degree black belt along the way in China where they attended the 1988 World Koshu Championships in Hong Kong. "She is my life, teaching and business partner and I attribute a lot of my success to her," he says. From the 80's to the 90's, Borkowski was also focused on sport Karate and competition as well as traditional Karate. There is a place for both in the world of Karate, and both are essential to development. Sport Karate is essential for young people to test themselves. NKS is focused on both and allows a pathway for students to move from one discipline to the other. Borkowski develops champions but is also a champion himself. A former internationally ranked competitor, he was six-time Canadian Champion. He was rated #1 by the North American Sport Karate Association (NASKA), the PKL, Karate Illustrated magazine and he has received hundreds of awards, trophies, and medals. Although all of these experiences were great and a valuable learning experience, ultimately Borkowski found himself consumed by it and made a decision to stop competing and reset. "I threw out all my trophies. This allowed me to reboot and start with a blank canvas," he says. This did wonders for him to reground himself in tradition and get his students to see that both are critical to learn for development of their overall ability to be great at Karate. "There needs to be balance. One should not be consumed by any specific side of learning Karate. There is value in all of it when used properly," says Borkowski.

At the end of the 90's Cezar started to develop himself in the business side of Karate as well. Not only was he a successful school owner, but he also became an avid writer, author, speaker, and teacher. In addition to writing several articles for a variety of martial arts publications, Borkowski authored Modern Shotokan Karate and co-authored the best-selling The Complete Idiot's Guide to Martial Arts. The books were a great success, especially the Idiot's guide. "I have always been able to take complex concepts and break them down into helpful lessons for beginners and that is exactly what this book was created to do," says Borkowski. It proved to be a great overview of Karate, but also other styles such as Aikido, Jiujitsu, and Kobudo as well as a great reference on how to effectively select a school and the benefits of training in the martial arts. Very well received, this book was rated highly on Amazon.com and other book sellers. He also worked to develop his research skills while learning how to write books. Doing so, he also researched and edited The History and Traditions of Okinawan Martial Arts and is currently working on translating and editing Mysteries of the Ryukyu Hand, which is a comprehensive take on the state of Okinawa Karate, the last of the true believers.

Borkowski also spent time developing his videotape credits by releasing a handful of highly regarded works to include Kobudo Weapons, Winning Point, Essential Okinawan Kobudo, The Master Class, and The Northern Karate System (NKS) which was a 15 DVD series. During this time, he got comfortable in front of the camera and did various interviews which then translated into features in magazines and speaking events worldwide. His lectures have also taken him home and abroad to talk about Karate, martial arts and many other related topics. Borkowski also developed his business acumen and online marketing skills by learning about the Internet, marketing and using social media so that in today's day and age, all he is able to leverage these platforms to continue his engagement with others. "I have a passion to teach others about Karate. The methods in which we do so are many these days and it's a gift that we can reach so many on these platforms," says Borkowski. "I want to leverage them and get the word out about NKS and the value of learning Karate."

As a dedicated practitioner with nearly 60 years studying, researching, and teaching martial arts there is no stopping Hanshi Borkowski. As the next two decades continued to provide ample opportunities to grow, he took advantage of every one of them. Always at the quest of improvement, he has visited Asia over 50 times in order to gain firsthand knowledge.

To this date, he holds very senior grades in Karate - Chito-ryu, Shorin-ryu, Goju-ryu. In Kobudo he is likely the only person in the world to hold rank and teaching licenses in Ryukyu, Matayoshi and Yamane systems (all received in Okinawa). He is also ranked in Jujutsu and Silat. This has all translated directly back to NKS. "What we teach in NKS is our RyuHa or pedagogical system," says Borkowski. "Our empty-hand curriculum, Seishinkan, is hybrid of traditional Okinawan systems infused with boxing, BJJ, stand-up and submission grappling and Silat. We focus less on branding or compartmentalizing it as one or a few styles and instead, view it as broad-based, organic and evolving system that is both classical and cutting edge. We take the fluid approach in our Kobudo program which includes Ryukyu, Matayoshi, Yamanne and Mura traditions that I've discovered while training with some of the best teachers in the world." The key to success is to always evolve and Borkowski made sure that this consistency in evolution is a big part of what he conveys in his teachings. "Continue to evolve or become extinct," he says. Today Borkowski is focused on continuing to not only evolve but forge new students in his system to grow to their highest potential. Still heavily involved in charity work, teaching, traveling, training, speaking and writing there is nothing slowing down this master of martial arts. What he has accomplished from such humble beginnings is something everyone should learn from and aspire to. To start from very little and build what he has should teach everyone that if you give it your best, dedicate to a cause, work extremely hard and never give up, great things can and will happen. What's next for Borkowski is to continue on with developing his legacy not only in the martial arts but elevating to one of martial arts most prominent figures of this time. "I seek to serve and will continue to do so. This is a calling and purpose," he says. Anyone lucky enough to know Hanshi Borkowski or work with him will know immediately that his service to martial arts, his students and his system is only the surface of the depths of this great man and his honorable legacy. His honor runs deep, much like his knowledge, skill, and care for those around him and that makes anyone in his circle extremely lucky indeed.

DAOS

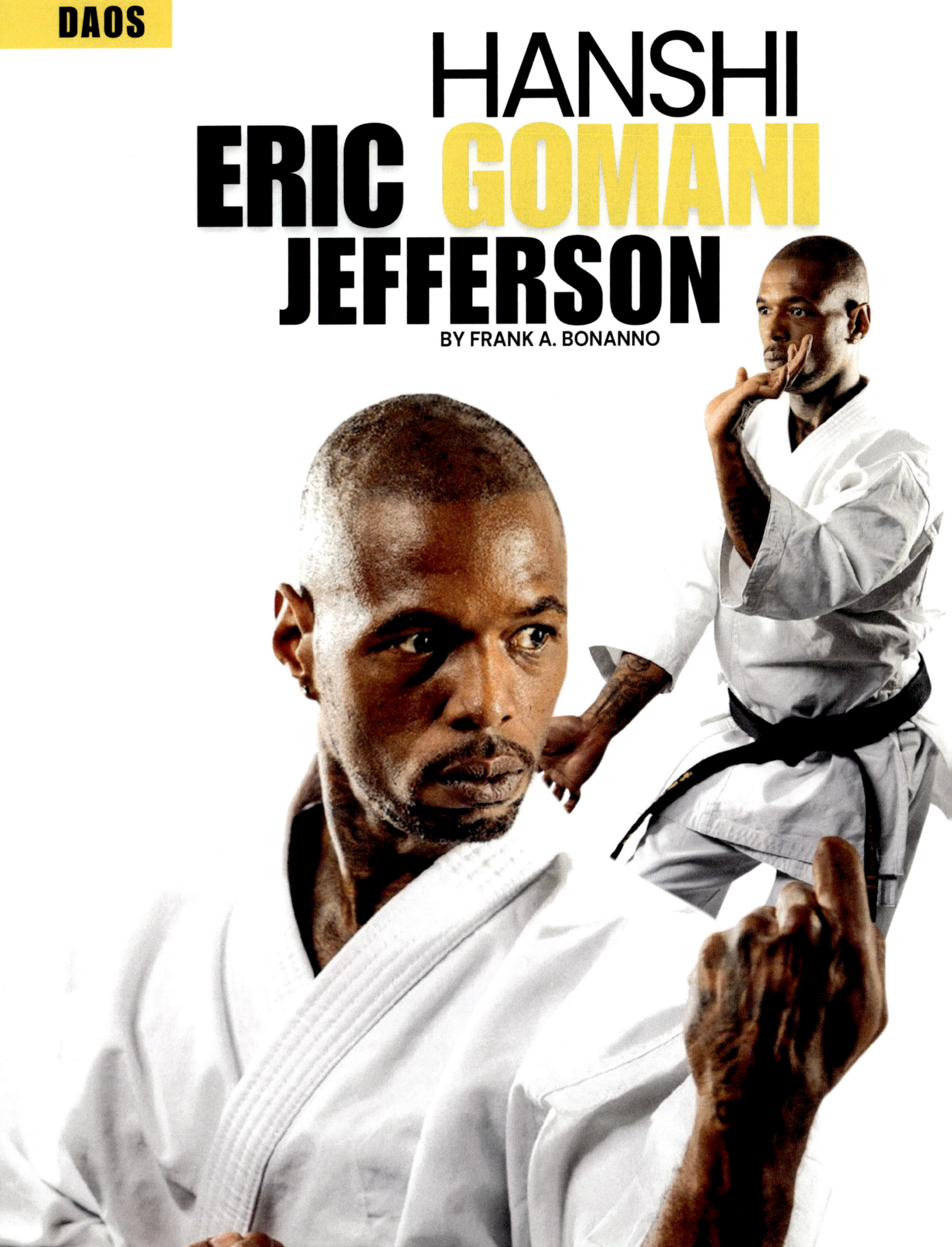

HANSHI
ERIC GOMANI
JEFFERSON

BY FRANK A. BONANNO

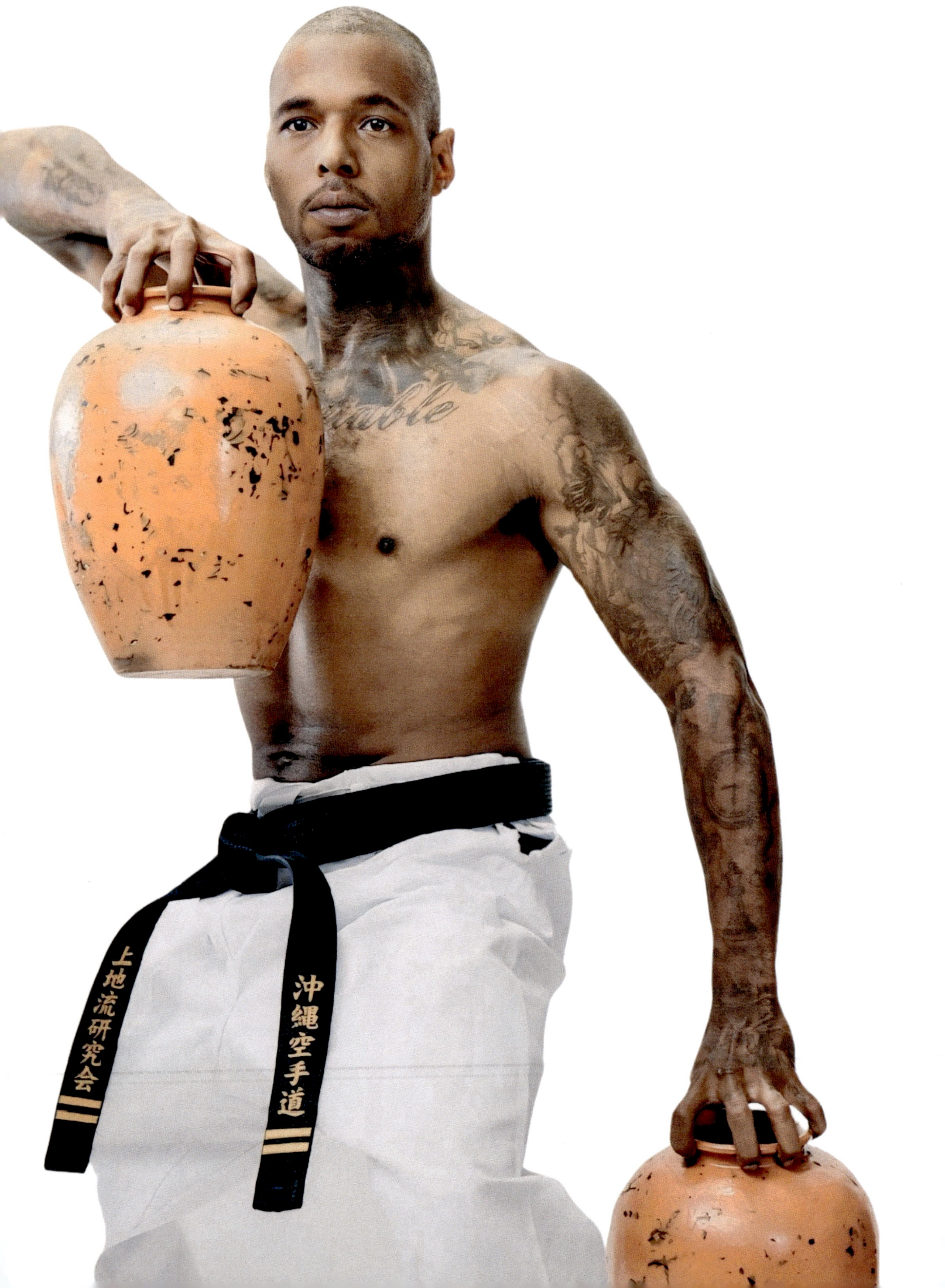
上地流研究会
沖縄空手道

"There is no one way to salvation, whatever the manner in which a man may proceed. All forms and variations are governed by the eternal intelligence of the Universe that enables a man to approach perfection. It may be in the arts of music and painting or it may be in commerce, law or medicine. It may be in the study of war or the study of peace. Each is as important as any other. Spiritual enlightenment through religious meditation such as Zen or in any other way is as viable and functional as any "way." .... A person should study as they see fit" -Miyamoto Musashi

A person should study as they see fit... Such a simple statement, is it not? Yet how many amongst us have had reins placed on our pursuits? Mixed martial arts and blending styles are all so cosmopolitan and commonplace now but it wasn't that long ago that students were dissuaded by their sensei from exploring the other arts around them. This ideology permeates every level of life to some extent. Society puts us all in boxes. Some of us may have the odd hobby here and there but to find people who are truly multi-disciplined is a rare thing. Most people just don't look that deeply, they find that one thing and their thirst is quenched. Some people never even go that far. Yet even four hundred years ago, Miyamoto Musashi was in the Japanese mountains extolling the virtues of being multidimensional. Why don't more people get that message? Why do people insist on confining themselves to one category, one way? More than that, why do people who are genuinely talented in one area think they won't be able to achieve that same success in another? 'Yes, I know how to design engines, but I could never play an instrument.' I have met countless people who have echoed these sentiments to me and it has always perplexed me. Life is out there just waiting for you to grab as much of it as you can, yet so many people walk around empty handed.

Gomani Eric Jefferson is not one such person. Quite conversely, Eric is a true "Renaissance Man," seeking out and sampling all that he can, constantly looking to further his knowledge and hone his skills. Jefferson is the archetype for life done well.

A native of Louisville Kentucky, where he still calls home, Sensei Jefferson began his martial arts journey with Shotokan Karate at the age of six. Having grown up without a father, his motivations were to be able to protect himself and his mother from harm and to learn to overcome his fear in the process. While perhaps not the most auspicious of beginnings, his love for the martial arts blossomed and he thrust himself into a myriad of arts including Chun Do Kwon TKD, Kupigani Ngumi (Afrocentric martial arts), Komasi stick fighting, Wing Chun Kung fu, Tai Chi, Mugai Ryu, Kobudo, Okinawan Ueichi Ryu, Pangannoon, Okinawan Goju Ryu, Shorei Goju, Silat, and Yemani Ryu Kobudo.

By the age of twelve, Jefferson sensei had begun competing, entering the Valentines Classic Competition. That day he took home first place in the nunchaku form and also competed in kata and fighting components. From thirteen onward, Jefferson has always competed. He became known on the circuit and gained a favorable reputation. Of his love of competition, Jefferson has said, "When I put my gi on and start moving and warming up, it's like heaven's gate opens up." As he pursued his love of competition, other passions began to take root as well. At the age of fifteen, while still just a green belt, Jefferson sensei had begun teaching karate at a local church community center. By the time he reached nineteen he had expanded to three different community centers as well as summer classes in an additional three locations for the parks and rec department of Louisville.

Concurrent to his teaching, training and teaching, Jefferson sensei was also pursuing his passions in the visual arts. After high school he attended the Hyatt Institute to study fine art with a focus on painting. Unfortunately, at age eighteen Eric lost his mother which led to him joining the Marines. While in boot camp, his drill instructors found out that he could draw and would ask him to design tattoos for them. Between that and skills as a martial artist, Eric began to curry favor among his instructors. Ultimately though, he was discharged from the Marines due to suffering from migraines. At the time he was very disappointed, but in hindsight he views the outcome as divine intervention.

As with his martial arts life, Eric's life as an artist also had its twists and turns. Having gone to school for fine art, his focus was in more traditional pathways such as showing art in galleries. His real dream though, was becoming an animator for Walt Disney Studios. He saw that as the best way to get his art out and seen around the world. Despite becoming popular for his tattoo designs in the corps, Jefferson held a negative view on tattooing, seeing it as something less than fine art. By his own accord tattooing was the furthest thing from his mind. That all changed when he met Travis King, a realism artist in the tattooing world. This opened his eyes to the possibilities and he was soon submitting his work to the revered local artist James Hardy in an effort to become an apprentice. Initially rejected, he was forced to sit back and take a look at his style. Eric realized that his style of art did not translate well into tattooing and needed to change.

Much the way one might examine and refine a martial technique that proves ineffective, Jefferson went back to the drawing board, revamped his style, resubmitted his work and was accepted as an apprentice. Unfortunately, his would-be mentor passed away a scant three days later. Though Eric only knew Hardy for a brief period of time, he left a massive impact on Jeffersonn's life and as an homage, he dubbed his home shop "Truth's Tattoos and Arts Emporium" paying tribute to Hardy's own "Body Art Emporium" while also announcing himself under his new moniker "Truth." When asked how the dichotomy between his martial arts self and visual artist self, Jefferson admitted it took a long time to reconcile those two facets of his personality but was eventually able to come to a place where they work synergistically, each one sharpening the other, sharpening him, sharpening all aspects of his life.

One might think that with a busy tattoo career as well as all his endeavors as a martial arts instructor, that Eric Jefferson's plate was quite full. However he has also maintained an active competition schedule as well, stepping up to the world stage in 2022 to compete in Scotland. When asked about his motivation to take such a big leap, Jefferson said he was interested in mixing it up with other hungry people from all over the world and pushing the boundaries. He also wanted to be recognized and known on the world stage. As for the difference between world competition and national levels, Jefferson Sensei notes that the room for error is almost non-existent while the level of everything else is higher- higher scrutiny, higher competition, higher levels of presentation and etiquette and higher level of humility amongst the competitors. Sensei Jefferson trains himself mind and body with intensity and laser focus to prepare for these competitions, then taking his training back to his students who in turn show him further ways to hone and dial in his own training creating a really beautiful symbiotic relationship.

Even with all his achievements and accomplishments, his thriving tattoo career, his many students, medals, accolades and distinctions, Sensei Jefferson is still reaching for more and has dreams of one day competing on the Okinawan stage, a space reserved for only Okinawan practitioners. He wants to stand where the forefathers of his arts have stood and compete with their ancestral lineage. Mr. Jefferson did ask that I mention his children as well, calling them the final component of all of this and wanting to acknowledge and thank them - Whilloe, Eric Jr, Kairo, and his step daughter Milli.

One thing that came up again and again was Sensei Jefferson's desire to become known, whether that be through his artistry or his martial arts prowess, he wants his name out there. We should know him, we should know his name and his story. Life is life, as you all well know. It is a perennial grind and the hooks of obligation and responsibility set in deep. Along the way people give up on dreams, make excuses or become complacent. Sometimes they achieve their primary goal and lose sight of their purpose, or give up on their hobbies because they're too tired. Jefferson, however, is the exception to this.

He has never stopped, never allowed his dreams and goals to get shoved to the periphery in support of the bills, and always strived for greatness despite the obstacles. As he has achieved his goals, he has set new ones for himself and then gone and gotten those as well.

This mindset has served him well and he has continued to overcome and achieve success across multiple fields, particularly ones which are definitely not the paths of least resistance. He has maintained his physical fitness, continued to sharpen and progress his skills, he remains dedicated to his students and runs his own business. He is the epitome of the virtues purported by Musashi centuries ago and an example to those around him. To push, to be well rounded, to stay hungry and always strive towards new challenges. These characteristics are in short supply in today's world of convenience and comfort. I believe that it is for these qualities that he should be known. After listening to him tell me his story, I believe his ultimate achievement is the life he has created for himself which is more than just the sum of its parts. We should learn from him and emulate his practices in whatever ways we can and we should know his name: Eric "Gomani" Jefferson.

SHIHAN
JOHN BUSTO

BY SENSEI ROBERT SHIMONSKI

It's funny how small things can lead to big life-changing events. For Shihan John Busto, it was a beloved childhood TV show called Kung Fu that started him down a path that would ultimately lead to a life spent building a martial arts empire. As John tried to navigate his way through school sports without sparking any real interest, it wasn't until watching his older sister JoAnn train in martial arts that he began to find his calling. "It was great to watch JoAnn doing Karate as it really motivated me to train," says Busto. Much like his martial arts heroes on TV showcasing supernatural abilities such as catching flying arrows with their bare hands and walking on rice paper without leaving a mark, he was hooked on learning how to emulate these same exciting skills.

Busto officially started training in Karate in 1980 at American Olympic Karate in Hicksville, NY where many martial arts legends originated. It was within these walls that a young man would begin his training with his first instructor, Sensei John McTernan. "He was a great instructor who focused on discipline, respect, positive self-talk, perseverance and resilience– all important qualities that helped shape who I am today," says Busto. At American Olympic, Sensei McTernan focused on Kenpo Karate as part of the Ed Parker and Al Tracy systems. "I am grateful for him starting me on my martial arts journey," says Busto. " As I participated in each class, I found out each day how martial arts not only helps one physically, but mentally as well."

Busto viewed martial arts as a journey even at a young age. It was this maturity that allowed him to move up the ranks quickly. Through the classes at American Olympic, he began to focus himself on mastering the curriculum and practicing constantly. At the age of fourteen, he received his black belt in Kenpo Karate. "It was a grueling closed-door test that lasted hours where I had to demonstrate self-defense techniques and sparring with people more than twice my age," says Busto. "I was one of the youngest at my dojo to receive such a high achievement."

Once Busto received his black belt, he didn't stop there. He continued to learn more advanced curriculum, teach at American Olympic and develop his other skillsets. "Martial arts have always been about self-development and self-discovery, while promoting a disciplined and well-balanced lifestyle," says Busto. "It continued to draw me in by showing me how to tap into my internal being." As a new instructor, Sensei John was motivated to shine. "As a young black belt, I would look for all new information I could get. I would volunteer to help at the dojo anytime I could," says Busto. "When teaching, I was always learning. If you want a lesson, teach a lesson." As a young black belt, he consumed information not only from his instructor but also sought out more in the form of books, magazines and videotaped lessons. "I would read Karate magazines to gain information and learn about seminars and new martial artists. To advance my training, I would save up enough money to order VHS tapes on Kenpo and other systems," says Busto. "I would call Tracy headquarters and Grandmaster Al Tracy would answer the phone himself to my unknowing." Not aware of it at the time, Busto would eventually continue his advanced training and receive many of his advanced black belt degrees from Master Tracy himself.

While at American Olympic Sensei John continued to train but also teach as an instructor. "About the same time as receiving my Black Belt, The Karate Kid movie came out. There was an abundance of new students who wanted to join, and I was asked by my instructor to start teaching," says Busto. Three days a week, I would walk from school to the dojo to teach group classes and private lessons." Continuing this progression, he took the next step in his martial arts career in 1994 and at the age of 22, he purchased American Olympic from Master McTernan.

The same year that he purchased the studio, Busto began to expand the business by working directly with Grandmaster Tracy. After going to a Tracy business seminar, he was introduced to martial artists from around the world and as chance would have it, was introduced to his next main instructor and world champion, Bart Vale. From 1970 onward, Vale, a major player in Kenpo Karate, had expanded his own set of skills with wrestling, traveling to Japan and developing what is known as "Shootfighting,", a martial art that combines both striking and grappling.

Predating much of the UFC's fame, Busto was already engaged in learning this art directly from Vale in 1994. "In Vale's seminar, he taught a variety of submission holds and ended with full contact sparring with everyone who attended," says Busto. "This was a very humbling experience for all participants because grappling was not a commonly practiced discipline for karatekas or in the United States until the early 1990's. I was so intrigued by his material that I invited him to come to my studio in the summer of 1994 and felt a rush of excitement because he was my first guest instructor at a fully-packed event."

Since that seminar, Vale has been Busto's longest running instructor and that ultimately led him to be a part of Vale's instructor program. "Our relationship continued to evolve, with me eventually becoming a regional director for the Shootfighting Association and one of his top students," says Busto. "I helped assist him with articles in magazines, training videos, and seminars." Through this connection Busto began to grow his own brand of fighting with the inclusion of various styles built on a foundation of Kenpo.

While continuing to hone his skills in advanced Kenpo and Shootfighting, Busto continued building his school American Olympic. Since grappling was becoming more highly in demand, he had an edge. "Working with Bart Vale led to having high ranking martial artists from all different disciplines come to my studio to learn about grappling," says Busto. "During this time, I really honed my fighting skills by following Mr. Vale's teaching regime which is based in 'no theory and all application.' It is sparring with every student and addressing what needs to be taught and worked on as opposed to teaching a random technique." Shootfighting has become Busto's signature art throughout the martial arts community as there are not many who can say that they have practiced it or even mastered it for that matter. "Mr. Vale has been an incredible teacher, mentor, and friend to me throughout the years," says Busto. "I am blessed to have had the opportunity to train with him."

Another major step for Busto was to augment his current knowledge again with a new instructor he met at a Kenpo Gathering of the Eagles event in 1999. While at the event he was introduced to Sifu James Ibrao, who was one of the first black belts in Kenpo under Ed Parker. It was interesting for Busto to see how Sifu Ibrao had branched into the more traditional Chinese aspects of the Kenpo system and expanded on it. It wasn't long until he was training remotely with Sifu Ibrao and while visiting, was able to meet his instructor, James Wing Woo. Woo is a co-creator of some original Kenpo beginner forms that many Kenpoists learn today. As Busto continued his training, he wound up becoming the first person to earn a black belt within James' system. It was not long after when James passed away, but his lessons taught, legacy and system lives on in Busto's teachings.

In 2003, Busto changed the schoo'ls name to Busto's Martial Arts, which he felt was a better representation of himself and what the schools focus should be. Grounded firmly in Kenpo, he wanted to make sure that he captured all arts, not just one. In the years that followed, he continued to learn, grow as an individual martial artist, and develop the many students in his charge.

In 2009, Busto started training under GM Norman Sandler as a primary instructor. Norman is considered one of the leading experts in Kenpo in the country. "From the time I was a teenager, I had heard great things about him," says Busto. "In 2009, he contacted me to see if I would be interested in having his instructor, GM Gilbert Velez, teach a seminar at my school. I was thrilled to have the opportunity to work with these two legends of Kenpo." From that initial seminar, he started to train under Norman directly. He then decided to join Kenpo International which is a great worldwide community and training directly under Norman learning the American Kenpo system, which is an updated system that Ed Parker originally taught to the Tracy brothers in the late 1950's.

In 2010, Busto started to train directly under GM Zach Whitson. "I met Master Zach in 2010 which led to both Mr. Sandler and I training in his Counterpoint Tactical System; a combination of American Kenpo, Doce Pares and Pekiti Tirsia," says Busto. "At first, I saw this as supplemental material, but it is now a major component of my standard curriculum. Currently, I am training towards my 1st degree black belt under Master Whitson." Since the beginning, Shihan John Busto's focus has been on building his school and growing his student base and that focus continues today. "Throughout my career, I have students who have been training with me for many decades, with two of them having each opened a Busto's Martial Arts of their own. My students have seen how much their training has impacted their lives, and I now have the honor of teaching their children," says Busto. He spends much of his time providing oversight and advanced training to his blackbelts and instructors to make sure every generation that comes next has the core skills Busto himself learned back in the day.

"Self-defense is the core of our curriculum, but our primary goal is developing role models and leaders in and outside of martial arts," says Busto. He also makes sure that his instructors and students understand the value of giving back. This is to ensure that all involved are always focused on what matters most. "We do numerous monthly events such as bully prevention seminars, fundraisers, and annual picnics" he says. "Bringing the community together, uplifting my students, and having an effect on future generations is my biggest success."

Busto's next steps as a school owner and martial artist is to continue his mission of charity, build new skills and motivate his students. When asked about his future intentions he clearly knows that if you never give up on martial arts, it will never give up on you and learning is a lifelong pursuit. "Training is like putting money in the bank" he says, and luckily Shihan John Busto is constantly investing.

SHIHAN
TERRENCE BOWLIN

BY SHIHAN GLEN BECK

EVOLUTION

The evolution of anything is generally based on forward momentum, whether it's humanity or any other biological organism. However, it could also describe the growth of anything, such as an idea, a concept, or the building blocks of society.

The Evolution you're reading about is the continued growth of The Deadly Art of Survival Magazine, and specifically, our Warrior of the Velvet Rope column.

The WOTVRope section only focuses on 'true' martial artists who work in the nightlife and bodyguard sector. However, we will now leave behind the status quo and widen the spectrum of the security business and introduce others who bravely work as police officers, correctional officers, and those who have filled the ranks as military men and women from across the world.

DAOS = Evolution
Evolution = DAOS

WARRIORS
OF THE VELVET ROPE

I'm not sure if the kids of today still use it, but in New York, there was a saying, "Riding the train." It was used both figuratively and actually. Riding the train with someone meant that regardless of where you went or what problems you might face, your boy was down to "ride that train" with you. If it got ugly, then it got ugly, but you knew you had backup. Although very similar, the actual part meant that you were on the D, the M, the Q, the 6, or whatever train you generally rode underneath, above and across the city. The thing is, the trains ain't nothing to mess with; they are dangerous regardless of your fighting abilities. And while riding the train with your boy by your side, you knew you had backup. I spoke with a correctional officer friend and coworker of Terrance's. He was reluctant to say anything about their time working together, in fact, the only thing he spoke of was proper protocol. It was then that I knew beneath the polite speech and relaxed exterior of Shihan Bowlin was a "do whatever it takes" to get home to his family type of warrior. The second man I spoke with told a story of the realities of prison life and how, regardless of protocol, in order to survive, you must fight fire with fire. Of Terrence, he said, "he was 'that guy.'" In New York terms, Bowlin was described as the guy who rode the train with you. "As prisons go," he said, "the facility is a transitional prison for hard inmates; it was no joke, and neither is Shihan Bowlin."

Terrence was born in 1971 in Houston, Texas, which had a population of 1,756,000, and the family stayed there until 1973. After a family tragedy, he and Mom moved to Splendora, Texas, a town of no more than 500 residents. A place where he and his family were considered outsiders. They were originally hailing from Tannyhall, Texas, an equally small town where their family had lived for six generations. When they moved to Splendora, they were considered well-off since a year prior, Dad had purchased a 25-acre piece of land. Hardship seemed to follow young Terrence, starting with the unfortunate passing of Dad in '73. Since the loss of his father, the lands have since dwindled to about 4 acres as Mom had to sell some of it off to stay afloat. It didn't take long before he began to know the effects of "ism," this being outsiderism, and was ostracized relentlessly for it. This treatment went on for years. He felt truly alone. By age five, Mom enrolled him in the Yabe Jiujitsu dojo under Sensei Jim Herman. Regardless of his training, Terrance silently endured the bullying. His lack of confidence enveloped him in a cocoon of worry and doubt. Even after years of training, he was still dealing with being picked on and beaten up. Eventually, he spoke to his sensei about it. The conversation was like a light switch had been turned on. Things changed, and he began fighting back, but his pent-up frustration poured out over the next few years. He not only won the fights that others had started with him, but now he was looking for trouble, even hoping for it. Eventually, he sought out fights and taught a lesson to every kid who ostracized him and had become a bully himself. Luckily, he grew out of it, but not before breaking the knee of the captain of the football team in 1983. Times were different, and as he explained- it was a hick town, and all he received was after-school detention for it.

The following year, in '84, he tested for and received his 1st dan. While he did very little competing back then, he became proficient in the katana, which he trained in for many years. In '91, he was in a car accident that afforded him a broken hip and femur, injuries which followed him throughout the rest of his life. While it stifled his training, he eventually returned to the arts later in life. In late 1992, he began working for a private security company, doing car patrols and alarm responses. He stayed there until 1997, when he switched careers and became a plumber for many years. Terrence's training continued, but his injuries took a toll on him.

However, much like all real men, he pushed through the pain. During this second time in the arts he became aware of other disciplines and expanded his interests. In 2007, he became a Texas State Correctional Officer. He was placed at a transitional facility at the James H. Byrd Unit in Huntsville, Texas. Every prison, regardless of the security level, can be dangerous; the Byrd Unit, however, has the distinct pleasure of housing some of the worst prisoners in all of Texas. Many are death row offenders, life without the possibility of parole inmates, and sex offenders. Since these are the worst that society has to offer, and they literally have little to nothing to live for, the guards are in a constant state of preparedness. The "life is cheap" quote is especially noted in facilities like the Byrd Unit, where the guard/prisoner ratio was 12 to 1032. The prisoners are not housed at the unit permanently, and they are eventually moved to another prison within a few weeks to months. Units housing prisoners of this caliber are given very little in the way of comfort. Their daily allowance of "free time" -how ironic- is 30 minutes for showers, 30 minutes for chow, and 30 more for lawyers or medical. A maximum of 90 minutes at best each day. There was also no "yard time," even if they had a yard, which they didn't. These conditions made a poisonous meal to digest for both prisoners and guards alike.

In the ten years that Officer Bowlin worked there he tried to keep within the boundaries of "protocol" when it came to disciplining inmates. Yet, these weren't school marms he was dealing with, and from time to time, he had to get his hands dirty. Each time, his martial arts training came to the fore while defending himself.

One day after chow, while he was escorting one of the lifers to his "house." Dragging along, he stopped at every cell to leisurely chat with other inmates, purposely delaying his lockup. Bowlin kept ushering him forward, and the inmate took offense to it more each time.

Life - home life, along with the daily grind and problems it affords, is a constant that floats in our head. Car payments, kids, wife, illnesses, and other bills were heavy on Officer Bowlin's mind as he moved the reluctant inmate forward. No longer an arm's length away, his face exploded in pain as a back elbow rocketed into his mouth and nose. A bright light filled his vision, and a life-and-death fight ensued.

By the time it was over, Bowlin was standing over the inmate who would spend what little time he had left to walk in the daylight or any other small joys that prison life might offer him, locked up and knowing that he lost the fight. He was face down in his cell with his arm torqued, and his shoulder, elbow, and wrist were locked in very awkward and painfully pressured positions. Bowlin's mouth was full of his own blood, which dripped down his face and onto his uniform. The sally port opened, and backup promptly arrived. The other officers had closed ranks protecting Bowlin and forced the other inmates back into their cells, which hadn't yet been locked. Days later, Terrence had permanently lost five teeth. The inmate was transferred, and he escaped what could have been a long and painful payback, something that Officer Bowlin wasn't known for. But he was still a force to be reckoned with, and every prisoner knew it that day.

Bowlin's longtime injuries forced him out of his job as time passed. His leg had become more of an issue than he'd ever thought it would. Understanding the life of a guard in a prison, he knew the inmates would target him every chance they could. He decided to take a position that was more clerk than officer for two years, which drove him mad due to boredom. The new placement was too much for him to bear, and he retired.

In 2012, before his leg hampered his movement, he worked as a bar/nightlife bouncer for some time. During his lifetime as a martial artist, he studied escrima and trained heavily in knife fighting. Shihan Bowlin, an 8th-degree jujitsu black belt, has a decades-long association with the Dekimasu Alliance and is the Regional Director in the Southwestern USA.

Today, Terrence Bowlin lives quietly in a gated community with his supportive, devoted, and lovely wife, Laura, and his two youngest children, Alex (14) and Ariya (11). He's also the father of two others, his eldest children Tatyana (28) and Jesse (26).

HANSHI KAMAU AKIL CHUKWUENEKA

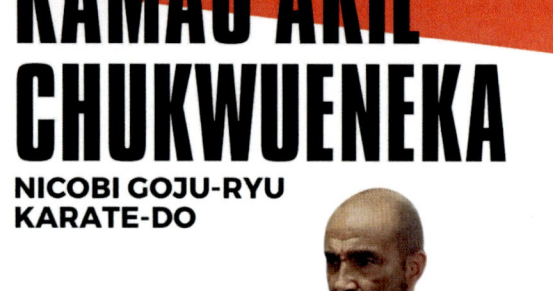

NICOBI GOJU-RYU KARATE-DO

OUR SERVICES
- Martial Arts
- Flexibility
- Cardio Training

CLASS HOURS
- Tuesday & Thursdays 6 pm
- Saturdays 11 am

JOIN NOW

(502) 944-1840

801 Dearborn Ave. Louisville, KY 40211

Chukwueneka@yahoo.com

- Want to ad MASSIVE value to your Martial Arts Program? Invest in this movement to help keep our Future Leaders out of the legal system.

- Master Samuel Scott, 14+ year Correctional Officer, has seen first-hand what happens when our teens follow the wrong person or crowd. He has committed 31yrs of his life teaching Martial Excellence to our Future Leaders.

- Be a part of the solution, invest in this life-saving book now.

Investment: 19.95 (Reg 24.95)

ORDER NOW AT: STAN.STORE/MASTERSCOTT

Street Law for Teens — What every GOOD cop wants YOUR teen to know about Street Law.

"I wish I had this extremely informative book when I was growing up. It would've saved me a lot of heartache and my parents a lot of money!"

SAMUEL SCOTT

少林流

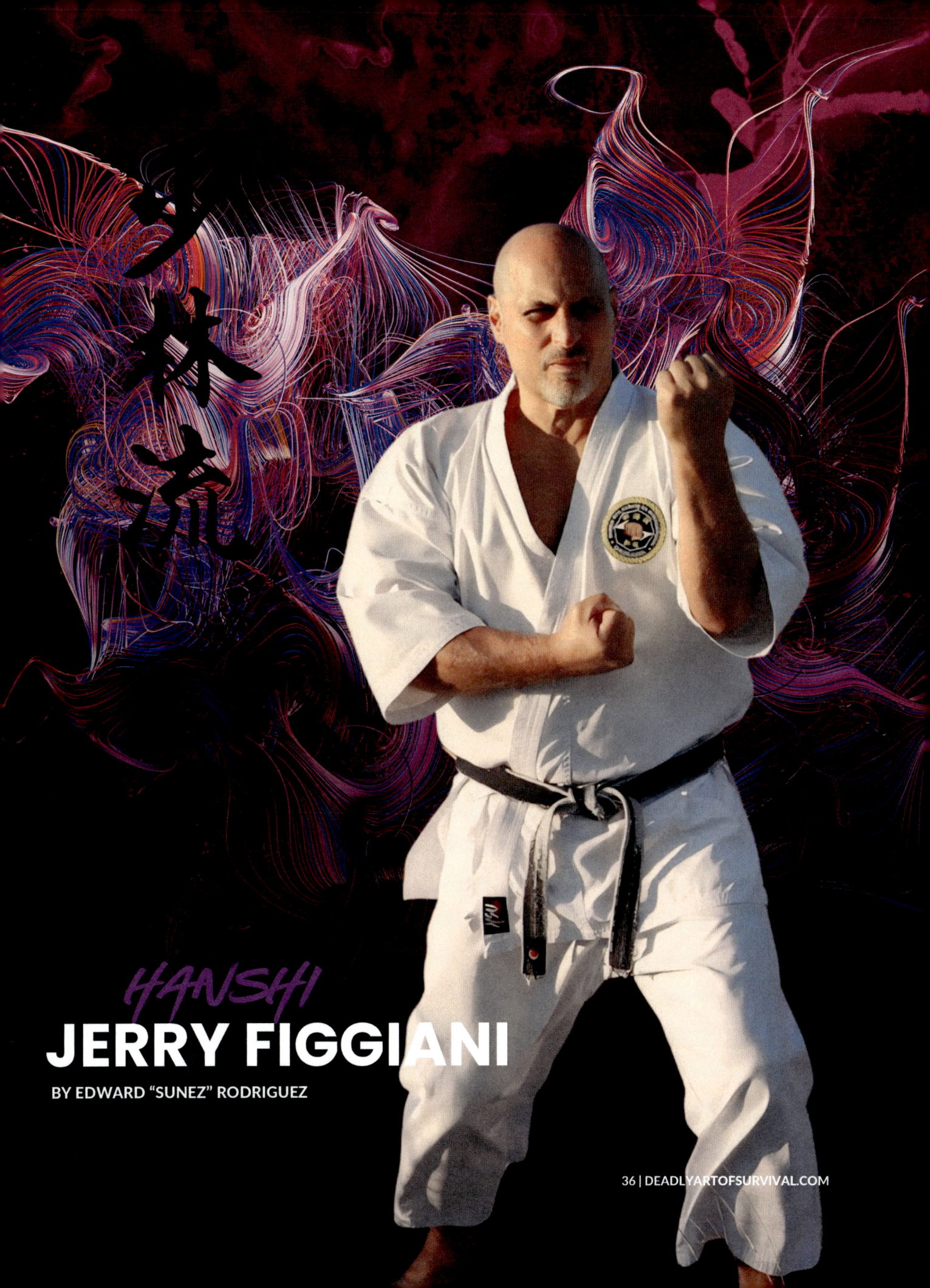

HANSHI
JERRY FIGGIANI

BY EDWARD "SUNEZ" RODRIGUEZ

36 | DEADLYARTOFSURVIVAL.COM

Insightful through injury, thankful through healing. Hopeful to willful when the mind matches the body. Exalted when the limbs perform the said motion in endless new ways. To prepare, to defend, to fight so well one may will a peaceful life. Martial arts is an endless cipher around these principles and actions where some are blessed to receive the honor of its full blessings.

Sensei Jerry Figgiani, 65 years old, attained these blessing when he recently received the 9th-degree black belt from the Matsubayashi Shogen Ryu Karate-Do Association. Presided over by the highest-ranking student of Shōshin Nagamine, Sensei Tamaki Takeshi, it was held at the Tokashiki Dojo in Naha, Okinawa: the Okinawa, Japan that is the birthplace of Karate.

This long road for Sensei Figgiani starts at his birthplace of New York City's Greenwich village and where he grew up, Kew Gardens, Queens. As a youth first becoming enthralled with Karate learning an Okanagan style when he was allowed some sessions. Eventually, he countered and overcame difficulties in academics and being deaf in one ear by becoming a star running back for his high school leading them to the Suffolk County Championship. Soon he would meet his girlfriend, Annette, would become his wife, wonderfully so 41 years later. A back injury curtailed his football career but he started a new one. Engaging back in the martial arts intensely he was able to open the East Coast Black Belt Academy in 1990, which still runs today.

Studying many styles and disciplines of Karate, Judo and Taekwondo, he has taught and excelled with the system of Matsubayashi Shorin Ryu. How he chose this vast system was simple yet sublime, "I kind of fell into it. There was a dojo by my house. I happened to go in there with a friend one day, and we started taking lessons. I liked the feel of it for my body type. I'm 5 foot ten inches, about 220 pounds. Some of the other styles that I tried, like Taekwondo, when we would do the poomsae (the series of pre-arranged patterns of defense and attack movements in Taekwondo), I noticed there was a deep drop in the stances. The front stance was very long. Matsubayashi style deals with a lot of natural movement. Everything has a specific measurement according to your body type. Even the way we breathe is a natural way of breathing," says Figgiani.

Through a humility for emptiness in beginning journeys of learning he absorbed many disciplines of Moo Duk Kwan Taekwondo under Grandmaster Richard Shun as a white belt. Not the higher belt at which he could have started. A crucial test also impacted him greatly, "When I was up for my first test, he gave me a list of requirements that I needed. I noticed that I had to read a book. I never read in high school. I never applied myself. I didn't want to do this. I wind up reading the book, Zen In The Martial Arts by Joe Hyams, and I really enjoyed it," says Figgiani. That propelled him to not only build a 1000 plus book library, but also author books as The Difference: A Mental Approach to Martial Arts, published in 2017.

The literature supplemented his martial arts journey to "appreciate not only the physical, because that drew me in. I was angry and I liked the fighting aspect of it. I learned to control my anger and understand that the fight is really within oneself.

"Earlier in my career, in the late 80s, I was competing in tournaments. In 1995, I actually was the number one rated fighter for the Professional Karate League. In my division, I was inducted into the Professional Karate League Hall of Fame. However, moving forward, my philosophy is I don't attend tournaments anymore. I don't have my students competing because I really came to the realization that martial arts is to develop human potential, whatever that may be in a person, you know, whether it's more confidence, controlling your anger, learning how to deal with people, or becoming more respectful," he says.

He has become disappointed with the lack of principles and ethics being reflected in the tournament culture. "The most important decisions you'll make will be without a referee to control the situation. When a child goes out to school, in the street, in their community, there's no referee that's going to say stop for water, a point, or if somebody's in an armbar, or chokehold. You're not going to be able to tap out," says Figgiani. "So it's about getting my students to understand that the most important fight is the fight within yourself. Can you show respect? Can you show self-discipline? Do you have perseverance? Do you have that indomitable spirit where when things really go bad or you fall on your face, do you have that grit to get back up? And that's the direction I went with my teaching."

This direction's power and worth was no more evident in the story of Robert Aliano, a successful student of Figgiani who took a wrong direction once he began his collegiate studies at Quinnipiac University in November 2008. Aliano was struck by a car near his off-campus house in Connecticut. The traumatic brain injury he suffered culminated in being given a near fatal prognosis. His extensive rehabilitation led him back to Sensei Figgiani and the East Coast Black Belt Academy in Middle Island. Over ten years, Sensei's guidance and training methods have helped Aliano survive and make exceptional strides, now able to walk, complete his degree at Quinnipiac and receive a Black belt.

The pedagogical success Sensei Figgiani has had over 34 years is the depth in his approach to simplicity. "When I do seminars the one thing that divides us is the patch, because it's just human movement. When I drop down into what we call a jigotai, a wide open stance like shiko-dachi, and we do our chest punches, I don't look at the movement anymore the way it's labeled," says Figgiani. "I try to get my students to understand it's just human movement. With this punch, if somebody was grabbing me, I could still manage to do the same punch, the punching movement, by pulling underneath the arm of my opponent and pushing the shoulder, which would be the punching hand, creating an off-balance effect. And people will tell me it makes more sense, rather than hand coming back into the pocket."

The practicality he sees has developed over years of training with countless disciplines and exemplary teachers, "When I look at my karate techniques, I look at it as 90 percent grappling, 10 percent striking. All the movements contained within the kata are really for in-close fighting," says Figgiani. "I believe there is limited striking with some of the techniques that are given, especially in the blocking category of a syllabus. So I kind of look at the movements a lot differently." Much of this is expounded on in his 2019 DVD, Simplicity In Understanding Kata Bunkai.

Ultimately, Sensei Jerry Figgiani's learning is a worldwide accumulation and his teaching is universally applied. His East Coast Black Belt Academy it is built as a safe place. "Nobody's looking to hurt you here. But when you step foot outside, you better be taking your training seriously," says Figgiani. "How you train is kind of how you're going to react on the outside. If you don't take that approach, not only physically, but mentally as well, you're going to be in trouble." An understanding that is completely understood.

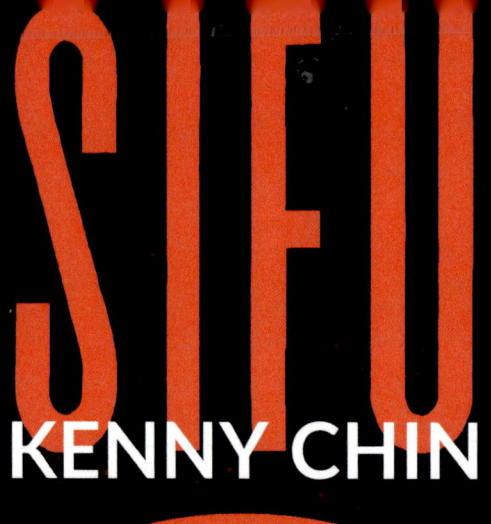

SIFU
KENNY CHIN

By Shihan Diane Wallander

You might have heard the phrase, "jack of all trades, master of none, but oftentimes better than master of one." The negative implication, of course, is that anyone who dabbles in too many skills fails to reach mastery in those endeavors. Yes, there are those who are laser-focused on a specific skill in their life and become highly proficient in it—and maybe not in much else- which is a beautiful thing. Although, there are those who seem to defy this idea. If one is fortunate enough to meet Sifu Kenny Chin and have the chance to listen to him describe the many aspects of his life—really, the richness and fullness of his life- the sense that one comes away with is mastery.

Born in 1951 in Hong Kong to a father who had trained in martial arts, Sifu Kenny Chin states, "Martial arts was in my blood, and it was sort of inevitable that I would learn kung fu." In Chinese culture, the practice of martial arts revolves around family, and the tradition was for young men to be trained by a hired master to protect family and community. Following this tradition, Chin's father learned kung fu, and Chin himself was strongly drawn to the martial arts. When he was only six, Chin's father went to the US to work. In the next ten years, young Kenny would see his father only a few times during visits to Hong Kong. As the oldest child in the family, Chin took on the responsibility for his younger siblings, instilling in him a strong commitment to his family.

Chin's first exposure to the art of kung fu resulted from his close relationship with his cousin Chin Yuk Din (he later took the name Dean Chin). Dean took Kenny to the Jow Ga kung fu shows that were common in Hong Kong, which is considered by many to be the mecca of Chinese martial arts. Intrigued by these demonstrations, he was able to seriously begin training in kung fu at age twelve under Grandmaster Chan Bud Yok, studying the Choy Li Fut and Eagle Claw styles. Fortunately, Grandmaster Chan's school was only two blocks away from the Chin family home—Sifu Kenny's mother preferred that he train close to home. The two cousins, Kenny and Dean, diverged in their training, as Dean focused on Jow Ga and later brought that same style to the Washington, DC, area, eventually becoming known as Master Dean Chin, the founder of Jow Ga Kung Fu in the US.

Sifu Chin had always been interested in films and acting, so at age 15, he answered an ad for actors in Hong Kong. He says that at that time, he was quite unfocused in school, knowing that he and his family would soon be moving to the US to join his father. Acting was a good diversion for him, and within a year, he had appeared in over 15 films in Hong Kong, so this diversion kept him quite busy during his last year in Hong Kong.

When Sifu Chin first came to New York at age 16, he had no intention of continuing his kung fu training. While in high school in Chinatown, Chin became friends with young men who were part of what Kenny calls the 'gangster world' in Chinatown. This gang was called the Flying Dragons, and Chin was asked to teach them kung fu, which he did for a short time. This life was not for him, so he left the gang on good terms and went to college, securing work as a computer programmer and analyst after graduating from City College of New York.

In 1974, Chin was approached in New York by a young woman in a karate uniform who was signing people up for martial arts classes. He went to see what was offered, and after being invited to take lessons, a young and brash Chin replied that he wasn't interested in being a student but rather would consider teaching for them

Chin was hired to teach kung fu at this school, and by a stroke of good luck, he taught with legendary Grandmaster Ron Van Clief. Chin has the greatest respect for GM Ron Van Clief, and they are still good friends to this day. He considers his experience teaching alongside the Black Dragon to be the most honorable of his martial arts career.

After a few years at this school, however, the business suddenly shut down—Chin remembers showing up to teach one day and finding the doors locked and the building dark. His students wanted to continue training with him, so he took the opportunity and began his kung fu program of his own. Life was hectic for him at this time, as Sifu Chin worked his day job as a computer programmer, then taught and trained in the evenings at schools he opened in New York and New Jersey. A man of many wants, he became a pilot, learned to scuba dive, and rode motorcycles. Chin even expanded his martial arts training when he met Grandmaster Woo Kai Mun, a 73-year-old Shaolin Master from China who took a liking to young Sifu Chin and guided him in advanced training in Northern Shaolin martial arts.

Chin was working as a consultant in New York when the 9/11 attack and its aftereffects impacted the entire region. He found himself out of work, looking for work to shift into. Chin did security work for a while. Then, a friend advised him to audition for a small part in the movie *The Interpreter*, starring Nicole Kidman and Sean Penn. Chin was hired and moved right back into the realm of acting, doing work in film, television, and commercials, becoming a SAG member, and was respected in the acting community.

Though many of his film and television roles have no connection to martial arts, Chin has done some stunt work, which was made possible by his martial arts training. In one role, Chin plays an older man who, while pushing a large garbage bin, experiences a heart attack and drops to the ground, dead. The film staff on set told him that they would create a very soft surface to fall on so that he would not be hurt as he fell. He responded by assuring them that it was unnecessary and then proceeded to demonstrate an effortless fall to the ground.

Long retired from teaching at a school, Chin continues to teach basic self-defense to anyone who wants to learn from him, including fellow actors and also seniors who are vulnerable to falls. He has great concerns about the level of bullying in our country and firmly believes that all youngsters should learn martial arts. He correctly reasons that a person with high self-esteem tends not to bully others, and those properly trained in martial arts are very likely to have this self-esteem.

Martial arts have always been, and will always be, a part of Sifu Kenny Chin's life. Throughout his life, Sifu Chin has applied the principles of respect, honor, discipline, and dignity that he has learned by training in the martial arts. When asked for his words of wisdom for others, his response is simple, elegant, and most fitting for this master of a man—a man whom some would call a 'renaissance man': "Be safe. Be healthy. Be with family."

RUNNING FIST KUNG FU
A modern perspective on ancient disciplines

RUNNING FIST IS A COMBINATION MARTIAL ARTS SYSTEM THAT IS TAUGHT THROUGH A SERIES OF CONCEPTS RATHER THAN A TECHNICAL APPROACH TO MARTIAL ARTS.

INCORPORATING ELEMENTS OF KUNG FU, KARATE, JIU-JITSU, PRACTITIONERS ARE ADEPT AT STRIKING, THROWING, TAKE DOWNS, JOINT LOCKS AND GRAPPLING.

While many have achieved ranks in Running Fist, this article follows on from the last two issues and highlights those who are actively instructing and committed to carrying on the legacy of Sijo James Robinson

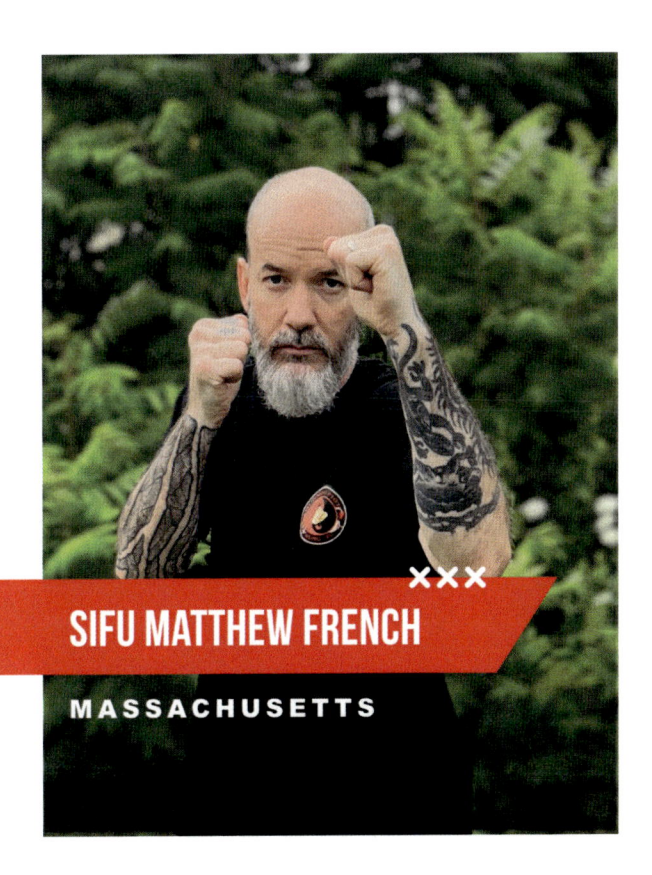

SIFU MATTHEW FRENCH
MASSACHUSETTS

SIFU MATTHEW began training in Running Fist Kung Fu under Sikung Lewis Henderson after years of living with debilitating back pain. Frustrated with the western medical approach to his condition, centering primarily on surgeries and pharmaceuticals, Matthew wanted to see if he could restore his health another way. Sikung Henderson started him on a program of stretching, breathing and strengthening to help him regain flexibility and posture. Over time, medication that Matthew was dependent on for pain management began to be less necessary and ultimately, as training progressed, it was not necessary at all. Through his healing journey Matthew discovered his passion for martial arts, trained hard and earned the rank of Sifu.

For him, Running Fist Kung Fu has always been about bettering the self in mind, body and spirit for the purpose of self defense and self care. As such, Matthew has broadened his education to include training in NRA Self Defense Firearms courses and Civilian Combatives programs that are based on programs currently used by the U.S. military.

He started Running Fist of Western Massachusetts to pay forward the years of dedication he received from Sikung Henderson. His school is specifically designed to build speed, power and confidence in one's self and in the techniques. He emphasizes a well-rounded education to include full understanding of the physical and mental aspects of combat, including the legal aspects potentially faced in today's world. His combative techniques include but are not limited to Running Fist Kung Fu, Mauy Thai and Western Boxing, BJJ as well as the understanding and implementation of firearms, pepperspray, stun guns, tasers, knives and bludgeoning weapons used in self-defense.

SIJE LORAINE'S journey into martial arts began by accident. Being in the right place at the right time. A friend needed someone to practice on. And she said Yes! "Little did I know the journey that was about to unfold", she recalls.

The biggest obstacle was fear and a lack of self-belief. "Memories of violence and bullying often arose in classes, and I knew that the only way to get over it was to keep going."

With the commitment and never-ending support of her instructor and partner, Sibak Lou Markstrom, the supportive Running Fist Family, and the unwavering belief of Sijo James Robinson, those limiting voices got quieter, fear lessened and, in its place, grew a stronger sense of self.

As a yoga practitioner for over 30 years, Loraine finds martial arts to be a perfect complement. She is a leading authority on yoga and yoga therapy for kids and teens and was named Australia's Yoga Professional of the Year in 2022.

Looking back, I began martial arts to help a friend. I stayed to help myself. Now, I train and teach for every girl who feels powerless, afraid, or experiences violence. I do it for all the women who show up in class, to grow, develop and gain confidence. I do it for my mind, and I do it because I LOVE it. It is a part of who I am.

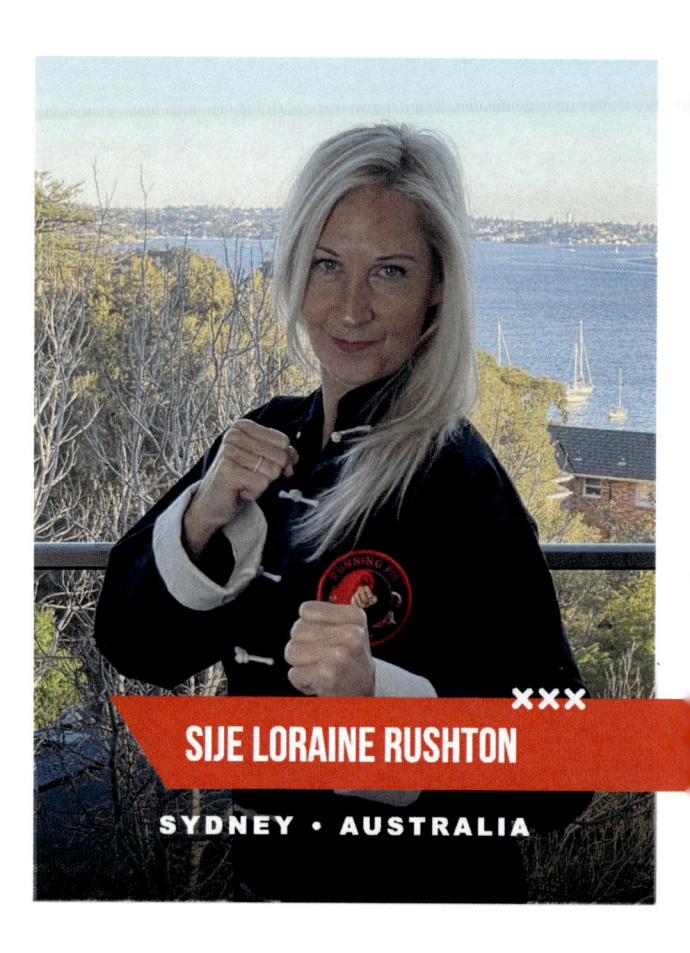

SIJE LORAINE RUSHTON
SYDNEY • AUSTRALIA

SIHING MIKE initially studied Wing Chun with talented Sifu Philip Warburton, who teaches from the Ip Man lineage.

This style fascinates Mike and led to him thinking about movement differently. Years later Mike was fortunate to meet inspiring Sibak Lou Markstrom and started with Running Fist Australia. Mike loves the flowing style of this concept-based approach and enjoys the ongoing refinement of learning to move in interesting ways. Mike continues training as he notices progress, increased body awareness and enjoys a sense of challenge and purpose. Mike says that the more he studies this art the more respect he has for its subtleties, and the dedication required to master them. Teaching has been a great way for Mike to develop his feel and understanding of Kung Fu.

He enjoys the community that has been created at Running Fist Australia. Mike teaches psychotherapy professionally and trains people to work in crisis support. Martial arts teaching is different; however, it has some common elements, such as presence, focus, engagement, aliveness, and connection. Mike loves that his wife Suma trains too and says it's a fun experience (mostly!). Mike feels very grateful to have met such passionate teachers and students along the way.

SIHING MICHAEL BURNS
SYDNEY • AUSTRALIA

SIHING HILVER LOPEZ
NEW YORK

SIHING HILVER has been training in martial arts for nearly 11 years and loves everything about it. As a child, he watched Bruce Lee movies and he dreamed of studying martial arts. This dream ignited a spark that he is following today.

As a child, Sihing lived in Mexico and there wasn't a way that he nor his parents could afford to pay for martial arts classes. When he was finally able to train, it made him so happy!

His childhood dreams came true which was an amazing feeling for him as he never thought or imagined it would be something he would actually accomplish. In addition to learning techniques, Hilver highlights that martial arts has taught him patience.

> "NOW THAT I AM OLDER, I LOVE IT EVEN MORE - IN ADDITION TO THE JOY IT GIVES ME, IT HELPS MY MENTAL AND PHYSICAL HEALTH."

SIJE KIRA TAFT
VERMONT • MASSACHUSETTS

SIJE KIRA began her martial arts career in 2013 in the Vermont branch of Running Fist under the care and instruction of Sikung Lewis Henderson. Currently, she trains under Sifu Matthew French in the Massachusetts branch.

What started out as a journey of artistic inspiration quickly developed into a love of all the sides of the art: The physical, spiritual, and mental.

Kira has persevered through many physical hardships, learning her body's limitations and how to adapt the art to circumvent those limits, striving to become the strongest version of herself. Her strength and will has gifted her the nickname "The Tank" from Sikung Henderson and her classmates.

The mental and spiritual journey has been the most rewarding aspect of the arts for her. Constantly in a battle against her own mind, she has taken to heart the adage "where the mind goes, the body will follow", and constantly pushes herself to overcome hardships and seek out new experiences.

Kira is grateful for all the opportunities martial arts has opened for her, as well as for all the instructors and friends she has made along the course of her journey.

BUSINESS DIRECTORY
FOR MARTIAL ARTS SCHOOLS & SMALL BUSINESSES

NEW YORK- LONG ISLAND
- Anthony Arango Martial Arts Institute 593 Broadway, Massapequa, NY 11758 +15167954102 http://www.arangowarrior.com

NEW YORK
- Soke Haisan Kaleak Police Community Center 127 Pennsylvania Avenue Brooklyn NY 11207 Training sessions Monday and Wednesday from 6 to 8 PM Phone (347) 723-2308

- Bill McCloud 759 Washington Avenue 2nd Fl Brooklyn, NY, 11238 (718) 210-3190 ninja70487@gmail.com

- Francisco Gomez New York Shuai Jiao (212) 548-6525
- Feliz Mejia Temple of nemesis gendai ju-jitsu 1585 Fulton street Brooklyn, New York, 11213 nemesisjiujitsu1@gmail.com

- Jessie Wray Next Level Martial Arts 501 E 163rd St, The Bronx, NY 10451 718 993 3344

MARYLAND
- Carl Matthews Faith Fighters Martial Arts Academy Christian karate 8502 Liberty Rd Randallstown, Maryland, 21133 (443) 286-9680 To God be the Glory
- Jerome Torres Blue Scorpion Dojo 7900 New Battle Grove Rd Dundalk, Maryland, 21222 (410) 905-5753 bluescorpiondojos@fmail.com
- Samuel Scott Full Circle Martial Arts Academy 9200 Alaking Ct. Capitol Hgts, MD, 20743 (301) 808-3578 info@fcmartialarts.com
- Shawn Ritchie Thurmont Academy Of Self Defense 202c east main street Thurmont, MD, 21788 (301) 271-3961 sanuces.tasd@gmail.com

CHICAGO
- Terrance Hicks Angelic Martial Arts systems 756 E. 82nd, 2nd Chicago, IL, 60626 (773) 661-8164 terrancehicksjr@yahoo.com

NEW JERSEY
- Victor Lashley Southpaw Gym - Boxing & Mixed Martial Arts 32 Hwy 35 Neptune, NJ, 07753 (732) 895-9422 southpawgymnjusa@gmail.com Victor Lashley Southpaw Gym 2.0 - Boxing & Mixed Martial Arts 1800 Lakewood Rd Toms River, NJ, 08755 (732) 895-9422 southpawgymnjusa@gmail.com
- GJ Torres Black Dragons Dojo Headquarters, 12 Main Street Eatontown, Nj, 07724 (732) 693-4409 blackdragonsdojo@yahoo.com Damien Wright Wright Fight Concepts 126 Evergreen Road, New Egypt, NJ. 08533 (732) 877-4041

COLORADO
- Brian Kiesel Running Fist Kung Fu Colorado Waterford Lane Fort Collins, Colorado 80525 Brian@runningfistkungfu.com

KENTUCKY
- Kamau Chukwueneka Nicobi Goju-Ryu Karate-Do 801 Dearborn Ave Louisville, KY (502) 994 1840 ChukwuenekaDAOSKYREP@yahoo.com

UPSTATE NY
- Tony Watts Total Wing Chun Jiu Jitsu Ryu Academy 200 N Water Street Peekskill, New York, 10566 (914) 468-3315

GARY, INDIANA
- Kamal Minkah 1975 Jefferson Street Gary, Indiana, 46407 (219) 805-5977 Kamalminkah70@gmail.com

FLORIDA
- Walter Evans Shihan School of Survival P.O. 213 Clearwater, Florida, 33757 (727) 641-0127 shihanwalter@yahoo.com

- Fernando Figueroa MARTIAL ARTISTS AGAINST TRAFFICKING 8374 Nw 64th St, JP-270965 Miami, FL, 33195 (829) 297-7807 fernando@antitraffickingbureau.org

- Jim Rivera Owaza Martial Arts 14726 county line rd Spring Hill, Florida, 34610

MASSACHUSETTS
- Barak Yalad Tenrai Seishitsu Dojo 391 Eastern Avenue Springfield, Ma, 01109 (Tenrai Seishitsu Dojo provides classes in the traditional Arts of the Samurai and Shinobi.) (347) 6620570

- Israel Lopez Sen-I Judo 2 Brookfield Rd Brimfield, MA 01010 (413) 279-4330 Sjudoclub@yahoo.com

ILLINOIS
Edward Carrillo Eagles Martial Arts System
- 2209 Mohican Road Waukegan, Illinois 60087 (847) 571-8490 emasrad@hotmail.com

PENNSYLVANIA
- GM Paul Cheng Martial Arts 1500 Garrett Rd A2 Upper Darby, PA 19080

CALIFORNIA
- Melissa "Alex" Medel 64 Movements (949) 444-4170 PO Box 393 Brisbane, CA, 94005 liveintaichi@gmail.com

AUSTRALIA
- Lou Markstrom Running Fist www.runningfist.com Manly Beach Sydney, Australia, 2095 +61 405559149

SMALL BUSINESS
- Peace of Mind Training CPR/AED/First Aid Training For humans and pets. Customized programs for Martial Arts school owners, wholesale distribution of AED's Active Shooter Threat Response Situational Awareness (631) 482-7900 www.POMT.org Lee@pomt.org

- Jon Meyer Auto Theft Buster 3280 Sunrise Highway Suite 320 Wantagh, NY 11793 (516) 557-4191 autotheftbuster@gmail.com

- Nychineselawyer.com law offices of Xuejie Wong pllc phone number (718) 461 - 8461

SHOGUN

SCAN HERE

DEADLY ART OF SURVIVAL
MAGAZINE DEADLYARTOFSURVIVAL.COM

Shogun
Jake Northfa$e - Official Song of The Deadly Art of Survival (Click Here To Listen)

02:12

imtappedin

REAL TALK
CHRONICLES
HOSTED BY
BILL FOSTER
ALSO ON YOUTUBE

BILLFOSTERONLINE.COM

JOIN THE CONVO

- ▶ LIVE PODCAST
- 📅 MONDAYS + WEDNESDAYS
- 🕐 7 PM - 9 PM ET

·Strength ·Self-Defense ·Self-Reliance 800k: Over 370 Pages, 24 Chapters Instruconal Manual Virtual Training & Cerficaons In Person Seminars & Certications

Call: 551-364-2545

Scan the Codes

STRENGTH
Kettlebell Secrets

SELF-DEFENSE
Survival Strong

A GUIDE TO STREET SURVIVAL & STRENGTH — PHIL ROSS M.S.